T.H.I.N.K. TO LEAD

T.H.I.N.K. To Lead

An Inside-Out Path to Mental Fitness & Sustainable High Performance

Dr. Khai Win

If you are currently experiencing severe distress, acute trauma, or symptoms requiring clinical care, Dr. Win strongly encourages you to seek support from a licensed mental health professional or medical provider. You deserve the right kind of support at the right time. Use of the information in this book is at the reader's own risk

Published by Game Changer Publishing

Paperback ISBN: 979-8-90158-401-9

Hardcover ISBN: 979-8-90158-037-0

Digital ISBN: 979-8-90158-038-7

www.GameChangerPublishing.com

In loving memory of Iri, the English bulldog, my brave little anchor.
A paw when I was breaking, a snort when I was spiraling, and yes…
the kind of farts that kept life honest.

For my parents, whose sacrifices opened doors.

For my sister, my shelter in the storms.

For Dan, my lifelong partner, who stayed close in my darkest moments.

And for you, the quiet fighters: I see you. I celebrate you.
May this book meet you in the middle of the battles no one applauds
and remind you that you're not alone. I am cheering for you.

READ THIS FIRST

This book was written for all of us. Now it's your turn. I want to hear from you. Let's connect.

Scan the QR Code here.

T.H.I.N.K. TO LEAD

AN INSIDE-OUT PATH TO MENTAL FITNESS & SUSTAINABLE HIGH PERFORMANCE

DR. KHAI WIN

FOREWORD

For more than a decade, my friend and colleague Dr. Khai Win has been helping clients discover and overcome hidden barriers that keep them from living their best lives. Her work as a neuroscientist and mental fitness coach in the areas of life and empowerment coaching has earned countless kudos from those who have experienced breakthroughs using her processes to attain sustained peak mental fitness.

Khai has codified these insights into THINK to Lead: An Inside-Out Path to Mental Fitness & Sustainable High Performance. This book lays out, in clear and concise language, the five-step process that smashes barriers to create emotional awareness and critical mindset shifts. Achieving this state is the foundation of everything we do, from how successful we are in our jobs and relationships with others to the most important relationship of all, the one we have with ourselves.

Using relatable examples backed by scientific neuro-research, this book teaches readers how to shift from simply surviving to creating a thriving framework based on strengthening positive thought patterns and emotional strength.

Dr. Win's THINK acronym is a memorable blueprint that is easy to understand and activate. "T" sets the table to track negative thoughts. Once identified, the "H" informs us to halt negative patterns. After we do so, the "I" challenges us to investigate hidden patterns. "N" begins our healing and growth as we nurture new perspectives. And "K" locks in those new perspectives by reminding us to keep growing by practicing what we've learned.

Khai and I both share a strong sense of the importance of setting an uncompromising standard to create transformational thinking and mental toughness. I go into these principles in my best-selling book, *The Standard*, which aligns in many ways with THINK to Lead. Both are designed for maximum individual flexibility and implementation that helps readers shift to an optimal dynamic and positive mindset.

Finding or reclaiming the best version of yourself does not happen by accident. It requires a disciplined approach using proven tactics and strategies to get the best possible outcomes. In that way, THINK to Lead is a well-thought-out game plan full of actionable steps, backed by years of experience and proven scientific principles.

This book is the blueprint you need to start immediately compounding important wins in your life. It is an essential read for anyone who is serious about stacking up those wins on their path to becoming the best version of who they are and who they were meant to be.

Ben Newman

USA Today Top 5 Performance Coach

2x Wall Street Journal Best-Selling Author

CONTENTS

PART ONE
SURVIVAL MODE

Introduction   3

1. **WHEN BREATHING BECOMES A CHOICE**   15
The Moment Everything Changed   15
When Life Strips Away Everything You Think
Matters   16
The Cruelest Lesson About Time and Distance   17
The Power Hidden in Every Breath and Choice   18
The Birth of a Life-Saving Mantra   20
The Science Behind Why Everything Feels So
Hard   21
Your Brain's Incredible Capacity for Healing   22
Your Next Breath Is Your Next Chance   24
Mental Fitness: The Training Nobody Talks   25
About Your Invitation to Breathe   26
Brain Notes: Inside the Survival Brain   28

2. **WHEN YOUR KITCHEN CATCHES FIRE**   31
The Night Everything Changed   31
7 Words That Burned Down My Mental
Kitchen   32
When Your Brain Thinks Everything Is Smoke   34
A Room of Your Own: Why That Matters to
Your Nervous System   35
When the System Drops You and Your Mind
Drops With It   35
People As Medicine, Not a Lecture   37
Men, Stigma, and the Weight You Don't Talk
About   38
How You Learn to Trust Your Kitchen Again   40
Brain Notes: The Brain on High Alert   42

PART TWO
THE QUIET REBUILD

3. **THE INVISIBLE ARCHIVES** 47

Your Brain-Body Ledger 47

Written in Our Cells: The Science of
Epigenetics 48

The Weight We Don't See 50

The Neuroscience of Trauma (and the Slow
Accumulation of Stress) 52

The Science of Healing 54

The Choice We Always Have 55

When Someone You Love Is Drowning 55

The Neutral Nature of Thoughts 57

The Invisible Wins 58

Brain Notes: How Stress Lives On 60

4. **THE POWER OF TINY STEPS** 63

When Everyone Thinks You're Fine (But
You're Barely Surviving) 63

When Trauma Hijacks Your Brain's Control 64
Room

Why Your New Year's Resolutions Keep 66
Failing (And What Actually Works)

The Woman Who Proved "Impossible" Is 69
Just an Opinion

The Man Who Forgot Everything but Never 70
Lost Joy 72

The Power of Invisible Wins 73

Your Journey Starts Right Here

Brain Notes: The Neuroscience of Tiny
Habits 75

PART THREE
THINK FRAMEWORK

5. **LETTER "T" – TRACK THE NEGATIVE THOUGHTS** 81

Catch the Loop Before It Catches You 81

7 Words That Shattered My World 82

Your Brain's Hidden Tax System 83

The Three Invisible Traps Stealing Your Life 84

The Debt I Didn't Know I Was Paying 85

The Emperor Who Mastered His Mind During
Chaos 86

The Silent Girl Who Found Her Voice 87

The Science of Taking Back Control 88

Your Invisible Win Starts With Awareness Small 89

Steps, Massive Freedom 90

Brain Notes: The Science of Thought Awareness 93

6. **LETTER "H" – HALT NEGATIVE PATTERNS** 97

When Toxic Mold Meets Toxic Thoughts 97

The Spiral Before the Storm 98

The Mountain of Rejection 99

When Your Brain Works Against You 100

Breaking Free: The Power of Pattern 101

Interruption Learning from History's Pattern
Interrupters 104

Your Personal Pattern Interrupter 105

Brain Notes: Breaking Thought Loops 111

7. **LETTER "I" – INVESTIGATE THE HIDDEN
PATTERNS** 115

That Nagging Feeling Something Isn't Right 115

The Hidden Stuff That Runs Our Lives 116

When Everything Finally Made Sense 117

The Science Behind Our Thought Patterns 120

Our Childhood Operating System 121

Why This Hits Men So Hard (And Why
Women Feel It Too) 123

Becoming a Thought Detective 125

Learning from History's Great Investigators 127

The Kitchen Counter of Your Mind 128

Your Investigation Protocol 129

Brain Notes: Brain Detective Network 131

8. **LETTER "N" – NURTURE NEW PERSPECTIVES** 135

When Your Carefully Built Life Crumbles 135

The Day I Overheard I'd Be "Just Another 136

Dropout" 5 A.M. Experiments: Turning an Insult into a Training Plan   137

From Muting to Nurturing (and How It Helped Me Later)   139

Stepping Outside My Bubble   142

The Neuroscience of a Growth Mindset   143

Helen Keller's Powerful Lesson   145

Remembering You're a Survivor (Your Turn)   146

Brain Notes: The Neuroscience of Perspective Shifts   150

9. **LETTER "K" – KEEP PRACTICING**   153

Your Brain's Incredible Renovation Project   153

The Dance Party in Your Head   154

Your Brain's Superhighway System   155

Clearing Space So the Strong Can Grow   156

Tiny Wins, Big Wiring   157

Learning from the Masters of Practice   157

Becoming the Boss of Your Thoughts (It's a Team Sport)   158

Your 30-Second Brain Workout   159

Fall Down. Rewire. Repeat.   162

Brain Notes: Your Brain's Renovation Project   167

PART FOUR
THINK IN ACTION

10. **THE FAMILY BLUEPRINT – HOW PAST HIJACKS PRESENT**   169

Your brain's old code: Childhood programming is still running the show.   169

David: "Why Do I Lose It Over Nothing?" Your   170

Brain's Secret Recording   172

A quick, grounded note on epigenetics   173

Your Invisible Operating System (OS)   174

How Your Old Code Shows Up   175

THINK: Your Reset Button (When Your Childhood Walks Into the Room)   178

Maya Angelou: When Silence Becomes Voice   181

What Rewiring Looks Like   182

Your New Beginning   183
Brain Notes: The Wiring Beneath Your Patterns   185

11. **THINK IN ACTION – LEADERSHIP**   187
Unconscious Bias: Breaking the Invisible
Chains   187
Your Brain Is Running a Program   190
You Didn't Write THINK: A Debiasing Skill,
Not a Personality Test   193
The Leadership Imperative: Beyond Awareness
to Action   201

12. **THINK IN ACTION – BURNOUT**   205
The Slow Boil: When Work Becomes Survival   205
Your Brain on Burnout   208
THINK in Action   212
The Personal Cost No One Talks About   216
The Organizational Cost Leaders Cannot
Afford to Ignore   217
The Burnout Imperative: From Survival to
Sustainability   218
The Culture Reset: What Leaders and Teams
Must Do Now   219

13. **THINK IN ACTION – TOXIC WORKPLACE**   221
When the Workplace Becomes a War Zone   221
The Neurological Hijacking of Workplace   225
Toxicity THINK in Action   227
The Workplace Toxicity Imperative: From
Survival to Reclamation   236
You were never the problem   237
My notes for the readers: Why This Work
Matters   238

PART FIVE
BEYOND THE INDIVIDUAL

14. **THE RIPPLE EFFECT STARTS WITH YOU**   243
How Your Smallest Moments Create the Biggest
Changes   243
Emotional Contagion: The Ripple You Didn't
Realize You Were Sending   244

Why Big Changes Feel Impossible (And What
Actually Works)   245
The Power of Going Micro   246
The Truth About How Change Really Happens   247
The THINK Framework: Your Daily Toolkit for
Creating Ripples   248
Your Micro-Action Journey   250
The Ripple That Starts With You   252

15. **LEADERSHIP AND COLLECTIVE CHANGE**   255

Upgrading Your Inner OS   255
The OS Nobody Talks About   256
You Are at the Frontier   257
Your Signal Is Already Broadcasting   258
Mental Fitness: Training the Inner OS   259
Recognition and Appreciation: Two Gears, One
Engine   260
Sleep: The Infrastructure Leaders Cannot
Shortchange   261
Psychological Safety: The Ground Floor   262
What This Looks Like at Scale   263
THINK at the Collective Level   264
The Invitation   265

Conclusion: Your Invisible Win Starts Now   267
Acknowledgments   275

PART ONE
SURVIVAL MODE

INTRODUCTION

THE HOSPITAL CHAIR

May 11, 2021. 3:47 a.m.

Fluorescent lights hum overhead while I half-sleep in a worn navy faux-leather hospital recliner, wedged between the machines and my mom's bed. I've been watching her heart rate, oxygen, and blood pressure for so long that the beeping has its own soundtrack in my head.

I'm supposed to be a high-performing professional. A **data scientist and project manager** in a big-name company. As a neuroscientist with a Ph.D., I understand how stress rewires the brain. My LinkedIn says things like *"high performance"* and *"brain health."*

But at this moment, I'm just a daughter in a hospital chair who can't remember the last time she truly rested. I jolt awake when the nurse comes in around eight a.m. to check my mom's blood sugar.

"Oh shit!" I blurted. She jumped.

I was supposed to be up at six. I have a 10 a.m. presentation. My laptop was balanced on my knees while the nurse adjusted my mom's IV. I was updating a deck, muting myself on the call every time a monitor beeped.

"Keep it together, Khai," I whispered. My title said "specialist/subject matter expert." My brain and body signaled *barely hanging on.*

THE AVALANCHE

Then the notifications started.

Slack from Ella, a senior colleague: *"Khai, I need you to fix this calculation error."*

Of course. Ella. The senior colleague who's been undermining me publicly in meetings for months, disparaging me and making me the scapegoat of all the things that could go wrong, and dumping the most tedious, messy tasks on me because I'm "detail-oriented."

Text from my partner: *"Don't forget, we need to talk about what happened yesterday."*

Perfect. Another fight waiting for me at home. My relationship fraying. My mother in pain. The project on fire because a teammate left without documentation, and I inherited the mess. A manager who treats Ella's behavior like the price of genius.

From the outside, I'm the reliable one. The "strong" one. The immigrant kid who learned English late and still became **the valedictorian, the Ph.D., and the data scientist** in the prestigious company.

Inside, I'm so freaking exhausted I can barely string thoughts together.

That evening, sitting in the hospital chair, a thought slides in, quiet and deadly:

What if I just… stopped? Stopped fighting, stopped breathing, stopped existing.

THE BREAKING POINT

The breaking point wasn't one big explosion. It wasn't just Ella's toxic bullying. It wasn't my partner's silence. It wasn't my mom's illness. It was a random Tuesday afternoon when I couldn't remember how to breathe.

For weeks, the suicidal thoughts stopped being visitors and started feeling like wedding planners.

How would my family manage? My sister can still take care of my mom. My partner will probably find someone who is "less complicated." And work? My colleagues will barely notice my absence. The world will continue unburdened.

The scariest part wasn't the thoughts themselves. It was how reasonable they sounded.

If you've ever had a thought like that, even for a split second, it doesn't make you weak or broken. It means your brain and body are screaming that something is deeply wrong, even while you're still telling everyone else, "*I'm fine.*"

Everyone tells you it takes courage to die. I think sometimes the real courage is deciding to live one more day. I had become what I feared most, a casualty of my own life. That's when I knew I needed professional help. I had to step away—from the toxic work, from the nonstop performing, from the version of "strength" that was killing me.

In that moment, "being strong" didn't mean pushing through. It meant stepping away. From the job. From the toxic cycle. From the battles eating me alive.

CRAWLING BACK

So, I did. There weren't cute Instagram captions or glowing selfies.

Intensive therapy sessions. Several rounds of **medication adjustments**. The exhausting trial-and-error of finding something my body could actually tolerate. My doctor kept saying, "*Give it a week; the side effects should subside.*" Sometimes they didn't, and we had to start over.

Sometimes stress and trauma knock your brain chemistry so far off-center that grit, gratitude lists, and "thinking positive" aren't enough; you need medical support just to get back to a baseline where any other tools can work.

This is where a lot of people quit, especially men who've been told their whole lives to tough it out, man up, or drink it off. You've been trained to see needing help as "weakness."

But staying in the process? Staying when everything feels hopeless, and you have no proof yet that it will get better, is one of the bravest things a human can do.

At first, it was messy as hell. Saying no when my whole life had trained me to say yes.

Letting my nervous system stop sprinting long enough to realize how exhausted I really was.

I also knew I needed something that wasn't data, code, or performance reviews. Something playful that reminded me I was more than my job.

So I took **Mark Rober's creative engineering class**. I built a ridiculous dog snack feeder. I spent hours researching drill bits and wood types instead of debugging codes or answering Slack messages at 11 p.m.

Holding that drill, I had a quiet realization:

Ella doesn't get to define who I am. My value is not up for a vote.

I had been so muted by toxicity that I forgot who I was. I forgot that my life *does* have meaning.

So does yours. Oh, bestie, let me tell you.

If you're reading this hanging on by a thread—like your worth has been slowly eroded by bosses, metrics, cultural expectations, or even your own thoughts—listen to me:
You're not weak. You're depleted. That's a wound, not a weakness. You need support, not shame.

THE REBUILD

When I finally returned to work, I wasn't "fixed." I was different.

I found a new role with a boss who actually saw me. I mentored others. I led projects. At one point, I was pulled aside to talk about becoming Interim Team Leader.

On paper, it looked like a comeback story.

But what changed me most wasn't the title. It was the anger I felt every time I thought about what had happened with Ella—and with every "Ella" I've met since.

Being silenced. Being made to feel invisible.

Being told, in a thousand subtle ways, that your brain, your accent, your background, and your needs are a problem instead of an asset.

I couldn't unsee it anymore.

Not in my team. Not in my old classrooms.

Not in the tech world or in the "little people" who keep organizations running while the executives chase metrics.

So I made myself a promise:

- Never again will I let a toxic culture decide my worth.
- Never again will I ignore the quiet suffering of the people without power in the room.
- Never again will I treat my mind like something I'm supposed to "push through" instead of something I have to **train** and **protect**.

Around the same time, my curiosity about what makes brains **thrive** sent me deep into high-performance science. I dove into Steven Kotler's *Zero to Dangerous* program, geeking out on the neuroscience of flow—those deep-focus states where time disappears, and you do your best work without frying your nervous system. I became a certified high-performance flow coach, layering that training on top of my neuroscience and data science background so I could help other high performers—engineers, analysts, leaders, founders, and caregivers—hit big goals without constantly burning themselves out.

For a while, it worked. I was leading projects, mentoring others, and stepping into more visible roles. I felt unstoppable. Until April 2023.

My mom was rushed to the ER at Lenox Hill. Suddenly, I wasn't just a high-performing data scientist and coach—I was a full-time caregiver again. The same old signs crept back in: sleep shrinking, irritability spiking, and that familiar darkness at the edge of my thoughts. Only this time, I saw it sooner. I stared it down and said, **"Not today, motherf*cker."**

THE REALIZATION

Even with everything I knew about brains, data and high performance, I couldn't outthink my own breakdown. I understood stress responses, burnout, and trauma. I could explain why panic attacks happen, why sleep and boundaries matter, and why "pushing through" backfires.

But in that hospital chair—first with my mom, then again in 2023—none of that stopped the 3 a.m. thoughts circling or my nervous system firing like I was under attack.

I was living proof of something uncomfortable: It's never about not knowing better. It's about brains stuck in survival mode, pushing us to perform, perfect, and appease until we lose our own center.

You already know the basics:

- Log off earlier.
- Say no sometimes.
- Ask for help.
- Don't tolerate disrespect.

But then real life shows up:

- If you're a **leader**, you tell your team to prioritize well-being—while your own brain whispers, *If I slow down, I'll lose credibility. If I show cracks, they'll lose respect for me*
- If you're an **individual contributor, coder, analyst, nurse, teacher, or frontline worker**, you sit through wellness talks—then you're back at your laptop at midnight because your mind insists, *If I don't overdeliver, I'm replaceable.*

My mentor Ben Newman discusses "The Standard" in his book, which refers to the level of excellence you hold yourself to and the non-negotiable commitment to present your best self, regardless of the circumstances. It's about consistency, discipline, and doing what you said you'd do even when motivation fades.

Here's what I discovered the hard way. You can't hold any healthy standard if your **inner script** is, *I matter only when I overperform. I'm safe only when I stay quiet. I'm lovable only when I don't need anything.*

That's the real gap. Between what you *know* and what your brain is actually trained to do under pressure.

Until you work at the level of thoughts, patterns, and tiny daily choices, the old wiring keeps winning. You don't need more information. You need a way to **train your inner world** so your outer life doesn't keep collapsing.

That gap is why this book exists.

WHY THIS BOOK EXISTS

Our brains are wired to scan for what's wrong. Criticism sticks. Praise slides off. We replay failures and ignore quiet wins. That wiring helped our ancestors survive real predators. Today, the "predators" are emails, meetings, metrics, biased bosses, broken systems, and old wounds we've never named.

Left on autopilot, that wiring can turn high performers into ghosts in their own lives.

This book grew out of the places where my own autopilot nearly killed me:

- Hospital chairs and hallway panic attacks
- A sexual assault dismissed with "we have more important cases"
- Therapy waitlists and canceled appointments
- Toxic colleagues excused because they're "brilliant"
- Suicidal thoughts that felt more rational than resting

The framework you'll meet here—called **"THINK"**—didn't come from a whiteboard. It came from:

- Nights I didn't want to be alive

- Micro-moments where I chose one more breath
- Hard conversations where I finally said, "No more."
- Coaching sessions with leaders and "little people" whose stories all rhymed with mine

Piece by piece, I turned it into something you can actually **use** when your mind is spiraling. THINK is my answer to my coach, Ben's challenge to:

Lead people with a tool so they can choose to change their behavior, not just sit through another inspiring talk.

THINK is a way to notice your thoughts, interrupt the old wiring, investigate the story, nurture a better one, and keep practicing until it becomes your new default.

When I first shared THINK on a big stage at a **Les Brown** event—800+ professionals, leaders, and change-makers in the audience—people came up afterward with tears in their eyes:

- "Thank you for making me feel seen."
- "Thank you for putting words to what I couldn't explain."
- "Thank you for giving me a tool, not just motivation."

That's when I knew this work wasn't just for me.

This book is for you if:
- You're a **leader, manager, founder, or executive** holding up a perfect facade while your inner world is on fire.
- You're an **engineer, coder, data scientist, analyst, caregiver, teacher, nurse, or frontline worker** who keeps everything running while feeling like you don't fully count.
- You're the "strong one" in your family or team—the dependable rock—who has quietly thought, I can't do this anymore.
- You've tried being "positive," tried grinding harder, maybe even tried therapy or medication—and you're tired of feeling like you're still failing at being okay.

This is **not** a book that tells you to just think happy thoughts.

It's not going to pretend you can breathe your way out of a toxic system without also making hard choices.

It *is* a book about:

- **Mental fitness**—training your brain like you'd train your body
- Your **Inner Leader Journey**—whether or not you have a title
- **Invisible wins**—the quiet, daily choices that nobody claps for but that still change your wiring
- Learning to become the **thinker** of your thoughts, not their victim

Whether you've already tried a bunch of strategies—self-help, leadership books, mindset tools—or you're just now admitting to yourself that something has to change, you belong here.

If you're skeptical of mindfulness and "soft skills" but know the current way isn't working, you belong here.

If you're a man who's been told to "man up" instead of speak up, you especially belong here.

This book won't tell you what to do about medication, diagnosis, or treatment decisions. That's between you and qualified professionals. What this book *will* do is help you understand how your **brain and nervous system** actually work under stress and pressure and give you **brain-friendly tools** you can practice in real life, whatever support system you choose around you.

In your most chaotic moments when you feel like you're just surviving, I want you to remember:

Even the smallest boundary, the quietest pause, or the honest "no" you whisper to yourself is an invisible win—and your brain still counts it.

Your brain is not fixed. Your patterns are not a life sentence. The question isn't whether you can change—you can.

The real question is…

Are you ready to **THINK** differently?

And reclaim the power you've been giving away?

Let's begin.

CHAPTER 1
WHEN BREATHING BECOMES A CHOICE

THE MOMENT EVERYTHING CHANGED

I t was a seemingly ordinary July morning in 2024. I was scrolling through LinkedIn, coffee in hand, when a post caught my attention. One of those LinkedIn influencers—you know the type, 200,000+ followers, engagement metrics through the roof—had been shadow-banned overnight. Gone. Just like that. All those followers, all that carefully curated content, all that digital validation… vanished.

We're all so obsessed with these metrics—views, impressions, engagement rates—these numerical validations of our worth. We spend hours building these digital empires, and they can vanish in a swipe.

This hit close to home. I'd been recovering from neck surgery, barely able to move, and had thrown myself into content creation as a way to feel productive, to provide value, and to matter in some measurable way. I was chasing the same metrics—likes, saves, and comments. That same digital validation. Wow, I had been focusing on the wrong things.

In this AI-dominated world, human connection—real, messy, imperfect connection—is what truly matters. Depth over breadth. Quality over quantity.

As this profound realization washed over me, my phone buzzed. A WhatsApp message from my mom: *"Call your dad. Your grandma passed away."*

Just like that—from contemplating lost followers to confronting actual loss. The universe has a twisted sense of timing.

WHEN LIFE STRIPS AWAY EVERYTHING YOU THINK MATTERS

I sat there, stunned into silence. My grandmother. She was a woman I hadn't seen in over 17 years. Since my mom, sister, and I moved to the U.S., we'd only spoken occasionally. She didn't own a phone. To hear her voice, she had to travel to someone else's house with a landline. We'd buy international calling cards and schedule rare, precious conversations.

And now she is gone.

How many of us live with that same quiet regret? The calls we didn't make, the visits we postponed, and the "I'll do it tomorrow" that never came?

We shove the truly important things to the margins while we chase the urgent—emails, deadlines, metrics, and other people's expectations.

I called my dad. My dad's voice broke as he answered, tears evident even through the phone. "How come you didn't tell me last week that Grandma broke her back and was in the hospital?" I asked, a mix of confusion and hurt washing over me.

I was infuriated. Just last week, he had visited me after my neck surgery, and not once did he mention that my grandmother was in critical condition with a broken back, lying in a hospital thousands of miles away.

THE CRUELEST LESSON ABOUT TIME AND DISTANCE

Back in Myanmar, my uncle FaceTimed my dad from the hospital. My grandmother was on a ventilator. Labored breathing. Machines everywhere. Each inhale, each exhale: a choice between staying and letting go.

On one of those calls, my uncle had panned the camera across her body, then abruptly said, "What's the point? Let us unplug and be done with it because I have other stuff that I need to do. I have to go back to another town."

He wasn't a villain. He was tired. Overwhelmed. Watching his mother suffer. Doing what he thought was merciful.

My dad, thousands of miles away in America, was desperate for more time, more information, and one last glimpse of his mother.

My grandmother didn't recognize my dad anymore. She was just trying to breathe, ready to let go but still holding on, perhaps hoping to speak to her granddaughters in America one last time.

And me? I was just... somewhere else. In my own recovery bubble. Trying to feel useful online. Feeling sorry for a shadow-banned influencer while my grandmother was literally fighting for every breath.

Nobody in this story is evil. Everyone is drowning in their own version of "too much."

That's the cruelty of distance and modern life: we are all in our own storms, so consumed by our pain that we forget someone in our life is taking their last breath.

THE POWER HIDDEN IN EVERY BREATH AND CHOICE

Through that FaceTime call, my dad watched his mother breathe with the help of a machine. Each inhale, each exhale: a choice between staying and letting go.

When I finally put the phone down, one thought hit me like a freight train:

Breathing is not automatic for everyone. For some people, every breath is work. And for some of us, in our darkest moments, breathing is a decision we're not sure we want to keep making.

If you've ever sat in your car in the parking lot, hands on the steering wheel, thinking, *I can't do another day of this,* you know that feeling. When breathing feels optional.

If you've been awake at 3:17 a.m., staring at the ceiling, thinking, *What's the point?* You know that feeling.

Imagining my dad watching my grandma fight for air through a screen opened my eyes in a way I wasn't ready for. It brought me back to a man whose words have followed me for years: Viktor Frankl.

Here was a man who, in 1942, found himself stripped of everything —his manuscript, his notes, his family, his dignity—in a Nazi concentration camp. As a psychiatrist, he watched his fellow prisoners navigate the razor-thin line between surviving another hour and surrendering to death.

What he discovered in those darkest places was that even when everything is taken away, we still have the power to choose how we respond to our circumstances.

In his seminal work, *Man's Search for Meaning*, Frankl wrote about prisoners who, despite starvation and torture, gave away their last piece of bread to someone hungrier. Nothing about their situation changed. Their internal choice did.

"Between stimulus and response, there is a space," he said. "In that space is our power to choose our response. In our response lies our growth and our freedom."

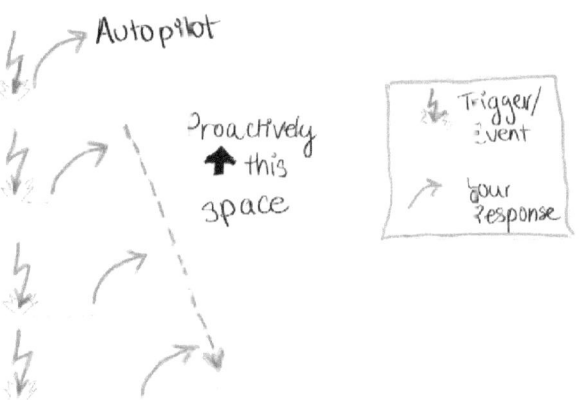

Think about that for a moment. On your worst day at work— when your boss is unreasonable, when the project fails, when you feel like you're drowning—there's still space to choose how you respond.

That space is tiny. But it's there. And inside that space lives the quietest, fiercest part of you.

THE BIRTH OF A LIFE-SAVING MANTRA

Thinking about what my dad had just witnessed and about Frankl, something clicked:

Sometimes the bravest thing you will ever do is simply take the next breath.

Not *fix your whole life*. Not *stay positive*. Not *crush your goals*.

Just. Breathe. Once. More.

That day, my personal mantra was born: **One breath at a time.**

Because when you're underwater mentally, "one day at a time" can feel impossible. Sometimes "one hour" is too big.

But one breath? One inhale, one exhale?

That's a rep most of us can still do, even when everything feels like it's collapsing.

So if you've ever thought,

- *I can't keep going.*
- *Everybody would be better off without me.*
- *I'm failing at home and at work.*

Then I want you to hear this:

Your invisible win today might simply be that you are still breathing.

Nobody posts that on LinkedIn. No one gives you a trophy for not quitting on yourself. But that is where mental strength starts—invisible and unglamorous.

We tell people, "It takes courage to quit your job, start a company, and take a big risk." True.

But it also takes a ridiculous amount of courage to:

- Stay when it's easier to disappear
- Breathe through the panic instead of numbing it
- Admit out loud, "I'm not okay," and still show up

Dying is easy. Giving up is easy.

Living—really living, breath by breath, when everything in you wants to stop—that's the hardest thing you will ever do.

And you're doing it.

THE SCIENCE BEHIND WHY EVERYTHING FEELS SO HARD

Let's break down what's actually happening in our brains when life punches us in the chest.

When we experience loss or trauma, our amygdala, the brain's emotional processing center, goes into overdrive. This ancient part of our brain doesn't distinguish between physical threats (e.g., a lion chasing you) and emotional ones (e.g., a breakup). The loss of a loved one, the loss of digital validation, the loss of identity—they all trigger the same primal response: fight, flight, freeze, fawn, or flop.

At the same time, your prefrontal cortex, the rational, thinking part of your brain, temporarily goes offline, and your body floods with stress hormones. Cortisol levels spike, your heart rate increases, and your breathing becomes shallow. This is why grief and trauma feel so physical—they literally change your body and brain chemistry.

YOUR BRAIN'S INCREDIBLE CAPACITY FOR HEALING

Now the hopeful part: your brain is remarkably plastic. Your brain is not a fixed machine. It's a living, changing, adapting organ. **Neuroplasticity** means your brain rewires based on what you repeatedly do. Your brain is forming new neural connections through your experience. It means you're not stuck in these patterns forever. Every time you:

- Take a slow, deliberate breath instead of firing off that angry reply
- Put your hand on your chest and name what you feel
- Text a friend, *"I'm not okay,"* instead of disappearing

… you are training your nervous system.

Think of your breath as your built-in "reset button." When you breathe slowly—especially with longer exhales—you send a signal through your **vagus nerve** (the superhighway between brain and body) that says, *We're not in immediate danger.*

That does a few powerful things:

- Activates your **parasympathetic system** (rest-and-digest mode)
- Lowers cortisol and brings your prefrontal cortex back online
- Widens that tiny space between stimulus and response

Researchers have found that even **a few minutes** of controlled breathing a day can:

- Reduce anxiety
- Increase heart-rate variability (a marker of resilience)
- Improve emotional regulation

You don't need incense. You don't have to sit cross-legged on a cushion.

If you're a guy reading this, thinking, *Breathing exercises aren't my thing,*

Let me translate: Slow breathing is a built-in performance tool.

- Before a hard conversation
- Before a presentation
- Before you walk in the door to your family after a brutal day

You can either let your amygdala run the show…

Or you can take 3–5 slow breaths and give your thinking brain a fighting chance.

That *is* mental strength.

YOUR NEXT BREATH IS YOUR NEXT CHANCE

My grandmother's final hours reminded me why I was still breathing. They also sharpened this truth: *Your next breath is your next chance.*

Not your next promotion.

Not your next achievement.

Not your next perfect habit streak.

Your next **breath**.

Your next breath is:

- The next opportunity to interrupt an old pattern
- The next opportunity to choose a different response
- The next opportunity to speak to yourself with 2 percent more kindness

You may not be able to change your circumstances today. You may not be able to fix your boss, your partner, your diagnosis, or your bank account.

But your next breath is yours.

You can use it to:

- Sigh in defeat
- Or inhale, pause, and say, "Not today, motherfucker."

Either way, that choice is an **internal rep**. That's the mental muscle we are strengthening.

24

MENTAL FITNESS: THE TRAINING NOBODY TALKS ABOUT

We train our bodies. We brag about steps, reps, and miles. But nobody hands you a program for training your **mind** under stress.

Mental fitness is exactly that:

Training your thought patterns. Training your emotional responses.

Training your nervous system to come back from the red zone faster

Not to become a robot.

To stay human—and not lose yourself—inside a world that constantly pulls you apart.

We wouldn't expect to bench-press 300 pounds the first time we walk into a gym. Yet we expect ourselves to:

- Lead under pressure
- Handle grief like a pro

- Take feedback like a champ
- Break generational patterns

… with zero training.

Mental fitness is not about never struggling. It's about building:

- A shorter recovery time
- A kinder inner voice
- A more stable sense of self when life hits

Throughout this book, the THINK framework is your training plan. Tiny, repeatable, science-backed reps for your brain.

Today, your mental "workout" might be as simple as:

- One slow breath before you answer that text
- Noticing one thought you usually ignore
- Naming one feeling in your body instead of bulldozing over it (like noticing, *My shoulder hurts today; I'm going to go lighter and take care of it, instead of forcing myself to lift 60 lbs.*)

That's it. Invisible reps. Real sustainable biological change.

YOUR INVITATION TO BREATHE

Sometimes healing doesn't start with a big declaration. It starts with a quiet decision:

I'm going to take one more breath.

Right now, wherever you are—on a train, in your office, in your car, hiding in the bathroom between meetings—try this with me:

Take a deep breath right now. Feel the air fill your lungs. Notice how your chest rises and falls.

This simple act—this choice to breathe—is where your power begins.

That's an invisible win. No one else saw it. But your nervous system did.

> You've made it through 100 percent of your hardest days so far, even the ones you were sure would break you. You're still here. You're still breathing.

That alone tells me something important about you:

You are stronger than you think. And you are not doing this alone anymore.

Your next breath is your next chance. Your next choice is your next opportunity to build the mental fitness that will carry you through whatever comes next.

Are you ready to learn how to breathe again?

BRAIN NOTES: INSIDE THE SURVIVAL BRAIN

Your Brain in Crisis Mode

When you experience shock or grief, your brain's threat response system activates immediately. The amygdala (your emotional alarm system) triggers a cascade of stress hormones, including cortisol and adrenaline. This isn't just an emotional reaction—it's a full-body physiological response that evolved to keep you alive in dangerous situations.

> **Try This**: When overwhelmed by grief or shock, place one hand on your chest and one on your belly. Take five slow breaths, focusing on the physical sensation of breathing. This simple act activates your vagus nerve, which helps regulate your autonomic nervous system and brings your prefrontal cortex back online.

The Breath-Brain Connection

Each breath you take directly impacts your brain function. When you're in crisis, your breathing typically becomes shallow and rapid, reducing oxygen flow to your prefrontal cortex, the part responsible for rational thinking and decision-making. This is why even simple choices feel impossible during intense grief or trauma.

> **Try this:** Practice "box breathing"—inhale for four counts, hold for four, exhale for four, and hold for four. This pattern has been shown to reduce cortisol levels and

increase activity in brain regions associated with emotional regulation.

Neuroplasticity in Action

Your brain physically changes in response to experience—a property called neuroplasticity. When you consciously choose to take that next breath despite overwhelming pain, you're literally creating new neural pathways. Each time you practice breathing through difficulty, these pathways strengthen, making resilience more accessible in future challenges.

> **Try this:** Create a "breath anchor," or a specific breathing pattern you practice daily when calm. During crisis moments, this familiar pattern becomes a neurological shortcut to activate your parasympathetic nervous system (your body's calming response).

The Social Brain's Need for Connection

Your brain is fundamentally social—isolation registers in the same brain regions as physical pain. This explains why loss can feel physically painful and why connection with others is crucial for healing. When someone witnesses our suffering, our nervous systems can actually synchronize, helping regulate overwhelming emotions.

> **Try This:** When supporting someone in crisis, match your breathing to theirs before gradually slowing your own. This non-verbal synchronization creates what neuroscientists call "co-regulation," a powerful way to help someone else's nervous system find balance.

CHAPTER 2
WHEN YOUR KITCHEN
CATCHES FIRE

THE NIGHT EVERYTHING CHANGED

S ome say trauma arrives like a thunderstorm. Mine came in a whisper.

It was a rainy night during graduate school. Water droplets poured down on me as I opened my eyes, disoriented and confused. I found myself on a park bench, outside, with no memory of how I'd gotten there. A terrible headache pounded through my skull as I tried to sit upright.

Reality felt distorted, like I was trapped in some episode of *American Horror Story*, caught in a twilight zone between consciousness and nightmare. I sat frozen on the bench, completely soaked, unable to recognize my surroundings. When I finally managed to move, I stumbled toward the main road, seeking shelter under the roof of a coffee shop.

With trembling hands, I found my boyfriend Dan's number and called him. "Can you pick me up? I don't know where I am."

Silence. His confusion was similar to mine, but we were confused for different reasons. Then he asked, "Can't you take an Uber home?"

What he couldn't understand was that I didn't even know how I'd gotten there—how could I find my way back?

When Dan arrived, our conversation revealed something shocking: we had been separated for quite some time. I had no recollection of it—no memory of what I'd been doing hours before, the night before, the weeks before. Nothing. The embarrassment of not remembering my own breakup silenced me. When he dropped me off at my apartment, I insisted I was fine, that I'd talk to him tomorrow. I just needed to be alone to sort through the fog in my mind.

Inside my apartment, my first instinct was to wash away the feeling of disgust that clung to my skin. As I sat in the tub, flashes of memory returned—fragments of sexual assault, physical violence— but nothing coherent enough to piece together.

That's when I realized my mistake. I shouldn't have showered. The evidence was gone. Any DNA that could have identified my attacker had been washed away.

7 WORDS THAT BURNED DOWN MY MENTAL KITCHEN

For three days, I locked myself away. I told my PhD supervisor at UPenn I was sick. The only person who knew anything was Dan, and even with him, I couldn't bring myself to share details. I barely understood myself. I didn't eat. I didn't leave. I just sat there, desperately trying to remember who had done this to me and what exactly it was that they'd done.

When I finally forced myself back to the lab, my colleague Nicola immediately sensed something was wrong but didn't pry—he simply offered me coffee cake from our favorite shop, the small gesture we shared during afternoon breaks.

Later, he gave me a hug and asked what he could do. That's when I broke down, tears flowing for reasons I couldn't fully articulate. All I knew was the pain, the confusion, and the terrifying gaps in my memory. When I told him about waking up on the bench, he convinced me to report what happened. Despite my reluctance, he promised to stay with me through every step.

At the police station, they performed a rape kit, and the detective assured me he would track down leads; however, it wasn't until weeks later that my phone rang.

"Hello, Ms. Win. There has been no lead for your attacker. Unfortunately, we have more important cases to handle and will be closing your case."

His voice was casual, as if discussing the weather.

Seven words. "We have more important cases to handle." **Seven words were enough to set my life on fire.**

You know that moment when you're cooking, and everything is perfect? The onions sizzle, you follow the recipe, and everything unfolds as planned—then you turn away for just a second, and suddenly the onions burn, smoke fills the air, and the alarm screams.

That's how trauma sneaks up. One moment, you're following life's recipe; the next, you're watching everything you worked for burn to ash.

WHEN YOUR BRAIN THINKS EVERYTHING IS SMOKE

Your brain is the most sophisticated security system ever built. And not just one alarm—it's a whole network of sensors talking to each other. In reality, dozens of circuits work together to keep you safe. But to keep this book simple and useful, I'll point to a few "stations" you'll hear about a lot: the survival stove (your brainstem), the feeling fridge (your limbic system, including the amygdala), and the "thinking counter" (your prefrontal cortex), with the hippocampus helping label time and place.

Before trauma, your brain works perfectly, triggering alarms for actual threats and staying quiet during harmless situations. After trauma, the wiring changes. Your stations stop communicating with each other. The "survival stove" heats up too fast. The "feeling fridge" locks and freezes everything. The "thinking counter" shrinks just when you need space most. The hippocampus can miss its time stamp, so memories come back as sharp fragments without a timeline.

But a burnt meal doesn't make you a bad cook—the stove just got too hot, setting off a chain reaction of protection.

Your brain tries to save you; we must teach it what is real fire and what is steam.

A ROOM OF YOUR OWN: WHY THAT MATTERS TO YOUR NERVOUS SYSTEM

Virginia Woolf said, *"A woman must have money and a room of her own."* People often use it in reference to creativity, but for her, it was also about survival.

At 13 years old, after her mother died, Woolf's once-safe home became dangerous when her half-brothers sexually abused her. Her childhood home suddenly became a battlefield, haunting her throughout life, as told through her writing and struggles with mental health. Safe spaces aren't a luxury but a necessity. Trauma makes our safe homes feel foreign. Some battles are invisible, but they're still real. Her insistence on having a room of her own wasn't just about physical space. It was about psychological sovereignty, the right to exist without invasion.

Safety is the fuel that expands your "thinking counter" again so you can actually cook, not just react to the alarm. You can't sauté feelings or plate decisions if the smoke alarm never shuts up. Like Woolf, you need a "room" of your own, too. Maybe it's a chair. A gym corner. A ten-minute walk. A truck cab with the engine idling. A place where your body learns, *I am safe here.*

This is how the alarm resets.

WHEN THE SYSTEM DROPS YOU AND YOUR MIND DROPS WITH IT

After hearing the detective's dismissal, hope vanished. The system was broken. I was told to see a therapist, but she kept canceling on me. After five canceled appointments, I gave up. What was the point? I lost faith in humanity, in myself, and in any reason to keep breathing.

I'd always been strong. Despite arriving in this country without speaking English, I set and achieved goals. At high school graduation, I watched the valedictorian speak and promised myself I'd be in that position at college, and I was—I set my mind to things and made them happen.

But my assault turned everything upside down. How could I "make it happen" when my world had shattered? What was the point of living in a broken system? Again, thoughts of ending my life invaded my mind. I no longer felt safe in my own apartment.

Nicola's kindness restored a sliver of hope. He offered company, made sure I was okay—even lent me his apartment while I figured things out. Sometimes, the only way out of a burning kitchen is to build a new one using our own tools.

Even though I understood trauma's neuroscience professionally, my knowledge vanished when I became the patient. When therapy failed me, I kept myself busy, as alone time with my thoughts was dangerous. Every quiet moment was filled with trauma, assault, and reminders of my insignificance. Some nights, sitting in my kitchen, I tried to consciously move forward by reminding myself what I'm made of by way of motivational speakers like Les Brown on YouTube.

One of my favorite Les Brown quotes is, "When life knocks you down, try to land on your back. Because if you can look up, you can get up."

I knew I needed to look up. I was looking up. But still, unwelcome thoughts kept following me. All I saw were dark clouds. *How the hell do I get back up when I don't even feel safe in my own thoughts?*

PEOPLE AS MEDICINE, NOT A LECTURE

I don't know where I would be without the small gestures from Dan and Nicola and from Josh, my graduate chair of neuroscience, who did something simple and human in a system that loves checklists.

We met for one afternoon. He brought his daughter. When he learned I didn't know how to ride a bike, he said, "Let's try." We went outside. They jogged alongside me while I wobbled, their hands steady on the seat, his daughter cheering.

I didn't learn to ride that day. That wasn't the point. The point was presence. No speeches. No grading. Just a steady hand on the seat that said, *You're not alone.*

One ordinary afternoon poured a little humanity back into a nervous system that had been living on smoke.

The scientific term for this is "co-regulation." Our nervous systems sync up. Sometimes you borrow someone else's calm until your own returns.

Josh's steady hand, his daughter's cheer, Nicola's coffee cake, Dan's ride—these were small acts that told my body a new story: *Someone comes for you. You are worth the trouble.*

Brains are networks built on repetition. Repeated moments of safety write new pathways. That's not fluff. That's biology.

MEN, STIGMA, AND THE WEIGHT YOU DON'T TALK ABOUT

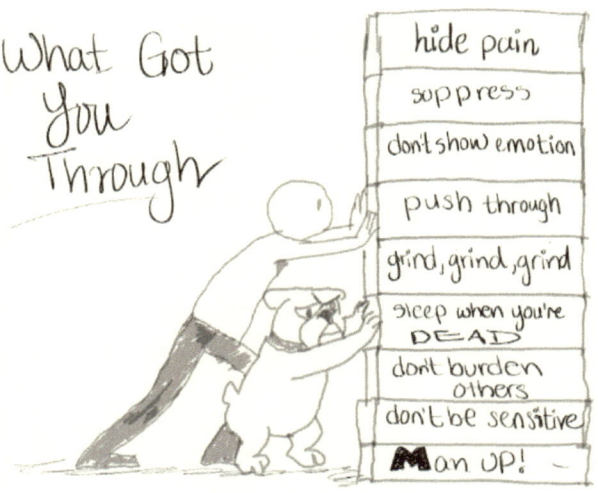

There was a man in our local fitness community—a strong, reliable guy who spotted others on heavy lifts. No one knew he was suffering in silence until the day he died by suicide. People kept saying, "I had no idea."

Let's be clear: stress doesn't discriminate. Men and women both feel the weight. The difference isn't in the feeling; it's in the expression. Men feel everything, but many have learned to swallow it, to say "I'm fine" when their mental kitchen is on fire, and to keep the mask tight even when it's suffocating them.

Stigma is heavy. It tells men to bottle it up, to "handle it," to fix it alone. But here's the thing about bottles—they explode when the pressure gets too high.

That "I'm fine" becomes toxic positivity in work boots. It's the same bullshit I fell for, wrapped in different packaging.

If you're a dad who jumps when your kid slams a door, a manager who snaps in meetings, a veteran whose heart sprints at fireworks, or a guy who can't sleep unless the TV whispers all night, you're not weak. Your brain learned to protect you. Now we need to help it learn to stand down.

The strongest thing you can do? Learn to say, "I'm not okay."

Not to everyone. Not all at once. But to someone.

Because white-knuckling makes the alarm louder, and your nervous system can't tell the difference between strength and suffocation.

Support doesn't always look like a heart-to-heart. It can be as simple as, like Josh did for me, showing up and holding the seat. Walking one lap. Sharing a sandwich. Sitting in silence. If you're the one hurting, letting someone jog beside you—even for one afternoon—counts.

You don't have to go through a "major trauma" to be worthy of care. Tiny traumas such as small cuts, daily stress, quiet humiliations, and the slow drip of not being seen add up. They live in your body and shape your reactions.

You can be both tough and tender with your nervous system. That's real strength. And sometimes the bravest thing you can say isn't "I'm fine," but "I'm not okay, and I need help figuring this out."

HOW YOU LEARN TO TRUST YOUR KITCHEN AGAIN

You're not cleaning up after a disaster—you're learning to cook in a new kitchen, your kitchen. While the smoke alarm might still ring at the wrong times, you're learning which alarms need attention and which can be quieted with gentle reminders of safety.

The truth about kitchens and healing is this: sometimes the most important ingredient isn't in the recipe. Sometimes it's just showing up. Hour after hour. Day after day. Believing in the recipe. Like Virginia Woolf writing through her darkness, we can create something meaningful from our pain, but it starts with learning to trust our kitchen again.

I learned the hard way how hopeless you can feel, no matter how big or small your painful experiences are. The one constant is being alone with your thoughts. When they swirl like smoke in your head, they're overwhelming. It took me years to understand and heal from my assault.

Trauma comes in whispers. It's an invisible weight. My negative thoughts stuck like burned food at the bottom of a pot. One cruel word could spoil an entire day. My brain kept cooking up worst-case scenarios even when the stove was off. I was trapped in my own mental prison.

But here's what I didn't know then, what would take years to discover: Just as every great chef masters their kitchen through practice and patience, we can learn to master our minds. What the detective never told me was that trauma doesn't just live in our memories—it lives in our cells, muscles, and DNA.

I learned that my body keeps perfect time with moments I wish to forget. They say the body keeps the score, but nobody explains how scoring works or how trauma rewrites not just your story but also your brain chemistry. Nobody tells you how your kitchen becomes foreign territory, how your reflection becomes a stranger, or how your cells remember what your mind tries to forget.

This is where my story intersects with science—where I learned that understanding the score doesn't mean you're losing the game. Sometimes, it means keeping your head above water, and that is enough.

There were nights I didn't think I'd see morning, moments when the weight felt too heavy to carry. But I'm here.

You don't need a "big story" to deserve help. Healing is practice: breathing, moving, naming, and letting people jog beside you while your balance returns. You're not trying to be your old self —you're building a wiser kitchen with better vents.

Are you ready to install better vents in your mental kitchen?

BRAIN NOTES: THE BRAIN ON HIGH ALERT

Memory Fragmentation

Trauma disrupts normal memory processing. Typically, your hippocampus, or your memory center, contextualizes experiences with time, place, and sequence. During trauma, excess stress hormones can impair hippocampal function, causing memories to be stored as disconnected sensory fragments rather than coherent narratives. This explains why trauma memories often feel present-tense and why details may be missing or disjointed.

> **Try This**: When fragmented memories surface, orient yourself to the present by naming five things you can see, four you can touch, three you can hear, two you can smell, and one you can taste. This grounding technique helps your brain distinguish between past and present.

Your Brain's Alarm System

After trauma, your amygdala, your threat detector, becomes hypervigilant, while connections to your prefrontal cortex, your rational thinking center, weaken. This creates a brain state where potential threats are identified faster but evaluated less accurately, explaining why harmless situations can trigger intense fear responses.

> **Try This**: When your internal alarm sounds, pause and ask, *Is this danger real or remembered?* This simple question acti-

vates your prefrontal cortex, helping restore the balance between your emotional and rational brain regions.

Neurochemical Imbalance

Trauma disrupts your brain's delicate chemical balance. It can deplete serotonin (mood regulation), increase norepinephrine (alertness), and alter dopamine pathways (reward and motivation). This neurochemical shift explains why trauma survivors often experience both hyperarousal (feeling constantly on edge) and emotional numbing.

> **Try This**: Regular physical movement—even gentle stretching—helps regulate these neurochemicals. Movement literally "shakes loose" stress hormones while promoting the release of endorphins and BDNF (brain-derived neurotrophic factor), which supports neural repair.

The Window of Tolerance

Your nervous system has an optimal zone called the "window of tolerance," where you can process experiences effectively. Trauma narrows this window, making it easier to slip into either hyperarousal (fight/flight) or hypoarousal (freeze/collapse). Understanding your personal window helps you recognize when you're leaving it and take steps to return to balance.

> **Try This**: Create a personal scale from 0 to 10, where 5 is your optimal zone, 10 is maximum activation, and 0 is complete shutdown. Check in with yourself throughout the

day: *Where am I on my scale right now?* This awareness is the first step in regulating your nervous system.

PART TWO
THE QUIET REBUILD

CHAPTER 3
THE INVISIBLE ARCHIVES

YOUR BRAIN-BODY LEDGER

They say time heals all wounds. Whoever "they" are, I'd like to have a word with them, preferably over coffee. Several cups. Because this conversation is going to need more than just a quick microwave minute.

Here's what most people don't tell you:

Your mind can "try" to move on. But your brain and body keep receipts.

It stores away every experience like a meticulous record-keeper, creating what I call your "invisible archives." Your nervous system stores *what happened and the contextual info that comes with it. How it smelled. How it sounded. How it felt*: the shallow breathing, the clenched jaw, the racing heart, and the split-second decision to shrink, smile, freeze, fight, or pretend you're fine. Your body records the moment your world changed... and then it replays it when something in the present rhymes with the past.

Not dusty boxes in the corner of your brain and body. But a whole filing system running through your cells, your muscles, your hormones, and your attention. And even how your genetic information is expressed.

WRITTEN IN OUR CELLS: THE SCIENCE OF EPIGENETICS

When trauma happens, it isn't only stored as a memory. It can show up as changes in how your body runs its internal settings, down to the cellular level, through a process called **epigenetics**. Don't let this term scare you away. Let's run through an example.

Think of your DNA as your grandmother's recipe for her famous cookies. The original recipe (your DNA) stays the same, but you add sticky notes (like *"Use less sugar after the diabetes scare"* or *"Double the vanilla after that perfect batch"*) based on your experience with making the recipe.

That harsh criticism that replays in your mind? It leaves a mark. The childhood humiliation that still makes your stomach clench?

It's there. The assault that divided your life into "before" and "after"? It's encoded in ways science is only beginning to understand.

Watch for danger. Last time we weren't safe.

Stay small. Taking up space costs too much.

These "sticky notes" are based on what you've lived through: highlights, margin scribbles, and tags that influence what gets turned up or turned down.

This is what scientists call **epigenetics** (literally meaning "above genetics"). It is the study of how your environment and experience can influence **how your genes are expressed**, without changing the DNA code itself. Your biology learns from life. It adapts. It tries to protect you.

It doesn't change your DNA sequence. It changes how your body reads it. And here's the most important part: many of these changes are **reversible**. Your story isn't set in stone. It's written in pencil, not in Sharpie.

Researchers studying the children of Holocaust survivors have found that severe, prolonged stress can be associated with measurable biological changes, such as differences in stress-hormone patterns and epigenetic "tags" on genes involved in regulating the stress response. Some studies even suggest these patterns can show up in the next generation, even though those children never experienced the camps themselves.

Not because trauma is "destiny," but because the stress system can be shaped by what a body has endured. Generational trauma can echo farther than we want it to. But so can healing.

Because if marks can be written, research suggests they can also be rewritten. Understanding this science isn't meant to trap you in a story of damage. It's meant to explain why your reactions can feel bigger than the moment—and why healing is real at the level of your body, not just your mindset.

This reminds me of Fanya Gottesfeld-Heller, who survived the Holocaust as a teenager in Ukraine. Her story reveals how trauma forces impossible choices—choices that reshape not just memory, but biology. Yet her survival also shows the kind of resilience that can live inside a human being even after the unthinkable.

As James Baldwin—the brilliant Black American novelist who wrote during the Civil Rights Movement—said, *"People are trapped in history, and history is trapped in them."* Baldwin knew this truth intimately. Born in Harlem in 1924, he experienced firsthand how trauma shaped not just individual lives but entire communities across generations. But Baldwin also understood that recognizing this truth was the beginning of transformation.

Your experiences have shaped you at the deepest cellular level, but they don't define your future. Every moment of healing, every act of self-compassion, and every step toward recovery is literally rewriting your story, one cell at a time.

THE WEIGHT WE DON'T SEE

You know those people who seem to have it all together? The ones who never miss a deadline, always look put-together, and somehow manage to remember everyone's birthday? I was that person, at least on the outside.

After my assault, I took medical leave from my PhD program, and I did what so many of us do when we don't feel safe inside our own heads: I stayed busy. I bartended. I smiled. I kept moving.

From the outside, I looked functional.

But inside?

My nervous system was on high alert. Sleep became an elusive stranger. My body would react before my mind could explain why: a sudden drop in the stomach, shoulders creeping up, breath catching when someone stood too close.

And if you've felt anything like that—if a Slack or Microsoft Teams notification on a Sunday makes your body panic... if someone's tone of voice flips a switch inside you... If your chest tightens before meetings, like your body is bracing for impact—please hear me:

These aren't "random reactions." They are your archive opening on its own.

Your body isn't being dramatic. It's being faithful to what it learned.

So when I interacted with people while bartending, the social connections temporarily masked my pain. My graduate program friends saw someone managing. What they didn't see was the water slowly boiling, about to spill over at any moment

Just because I was carrying it well, that didn't make it any less heavy. I wasn't thriving; I was surviving, and it was draining the color from every aspect of my life.

THE NEUROSCIENCE OF TRAUMA (AND THE SLOW ACCUMULATION OF STRESS)

Trauma doesn't just hurt. Trauma **reorganizes**.

When something overwhelms you and your system can't process it in real time, your brain prioritizes survival over storytelling.

A few key things can happen:

- The **amygdala** (threat detector) becomes more reactive, quicker to hit the alarm.
- The **prefrontal cortex** (your planning, perspective, and impulse-control "CEO") can go offline under stress.
- The **hippocampus** (context and time-stamping memory) may struggle to file the experience as "then," which is why traumatic memory can feel like "now."

It's your brain doing exactly what it evolved to do: protect you.

Society loves to misunderstand trauma survivors. They call PTSD "in your head." They call depression "lazy." They watch veterans struggle and ask why they can't "just move on."

What they don't understand is that many survivors aren't choosing the past. Their bodies are stuck in survival mode. The alarm stays loud. The system keeps scanning.

Our brain can learn to treat harmless cues like danger because they *match the pattern* of danger.

We're not choosing to relive it. Our nervous system is trying to prevent it.

This is trauma.   This is also trauma.   So is This.

And here's what makes it even trickier: not all trauma is a single explosion. Sometimes it's the slow drip. Sometimes it's a thousand small cuts.

Stress accumulates layer by layer—deadlines, caregiving, financial pressure, toxic workplaces, chronic criticism, and the daily effort of staying composed.

It's like wearing a backpack, and someone adds a small stone every day. At first, you adjust. Then you normalize. Then you stop noticing how heavy it is… until it starts costing you your sleep, your patience, your relationships, your joy, your health, and your ability to think clearly.

You don't notice the load building……

until you can't carry yourself Anymore

Scientists call this cumulative burden **allostatic load**: The long-term strain on the body when stress is constant and recovery is insufficient. Prolonged stress can affect memory, mood, immune function, inflammation, and even how your brain allocates attention. ***Your body pays attention to what your mouth tries to minimize.***

THE SCIENCE OF HEALING

But just as trauma can leave lasting imprints, so can our healing.

The most exciting discovery in neuroscience is neuroplasticity—your brain's ability to rewire itself throughout your entire life. Every time you practice a new skill, form a healthy relationship, or engage in healing activities, you're literally building new neural pathways. The brain that was shaped by trauma can be reshaped by recovery.

Studies show that interventions like meditation can reduce hyperactivity in the amygdala while strengthening the prefrontal cortex. Regular exercise doesn't just improve your physical health—it promotes the growth of new brain cells, particularly in areas damaged by chronic stress. Even simple practices like deep breathing can activate your parasympathetic nervous system, telling your body it's safe to rest and repair.

Trauma-informed therapies work by helping your brain distinguish between past and present. When you process traumatic memories in a safe environment, you're teaching your amygdala that the danger has passed. You're giving your prefrontal cortex the chance to come back online and regulate your emotions.

Consider Frida Kahlo, the iconic Mexican painter whose life was defined by physical suffering. After a devastating bus accident that shattered her body, doctors said she'd never walk again. Confined to her bed, Frida didn't just lie there—she painted what she couldn't "positive-think" her way out of.

Her father gave her a mirror, and she transformed her personal prison into an art studio. "I paint myself," she said, "because I'm often alone, and I am the subject I know best."

Frida's story illustrates something profound: even in our darkest moments, we have the power to create meaning from our pain. That doesn't erase the trauma, but it changes what trauma gets to rule. ***Meaning is not denial. Meaning is ownership.***

THE CHOICE WE ALWAYS HAVE

We don't choose what happens to us. We don't choose the families we're born into.

We don't choose the people who hurt us, dismiss us, betray us.

But we *do* have a choice in what we practice next.

Baldwin again: *"Not everything that is faced can be changed, but nothing can be changed until it is faced."*

Running kept me alive for a season. But running isn't the same as healing. One day, I realized I wasn't just surviving the assault. I was surviving my own archive—my own body's constant alarms.

And I wanted out.

WHEN SOMEONE YOU LOVE IS DROWNING

Maybe you're reading this thinking, *I haven't experienced severe trauma.*

Let me be clear: *pain is not a competition.*

Sometimes the drowning looks like depression. Sometimes it looks like rage. Sometimes it looks like a man who never cries but drinks more than he admits. Sometimes it looks like a high performer who can't sleep unless the TV is on because silence is too loud.

Sometimes it's the accumulation of smaller wounds, what Dr. Meg Arroll calls *"tiny traumas."* The chronic stress of a toxic workplace, growing up with a parent who was emotionally unavailable, and repeated experiences of feeling invisible or unheard.

And when someone you love is drowning in invisible pain, most people panic and shout advice from the shore: "Just think positive." "It could be worse." "Have you tried meditation?"

But a drowning person doesn't need a lecture. They need someone willing to **get soaked**, to step in anyway, and to stay close enough to help them float until they can breathe again.

Your nervous system can calm another nervous system. That's *co-regulation.*

Not your fixes. Not your comparisons. Just your willingness to sit in the discomfort with them, to bear witness without turning away. The most powerful words you can offer aren't "It will get better," but "I'm here, and I'm not going anywhere."

Your brain is wired for empathy. Mirror neurons fire when you see someone in pain, activating the same neural circuits as if you were experiencing that pain yourself. This isn't just emotional—it's biological. When you truly listen to someone's suffering, your nervous systems begin to synchronize. Your steady presence can literally help regulate their dysregulated system.

This is why connection heals. Not because it erases pain, but because it reminds us we don't have to carry it alone.

THE NEUTRAL NATURE OF THOUGHTS

It took me years to understand that thoughts themselves are neutral.

That was the distinction Joseph Nguyen made in his book *Don't Believe Everything You Think*. There is a difference between thoughts and thinking.

Thoughts are just mental events that pop up automatically, like bubbles rising to the surface of water. But thinking is what happens when we engage with those thoughts, when we grab onto them and start spinning stories around them.

A thought might be, *I'm not good enough.* But thinking turns that into, *I'm not good enough because I failed that presentation last week, and everyone probably thinks I'm incompetent, and I'll never get promoted, and my career is over.*

See the difference? One is a simple mental event. The other is the construction we've built around it.

Think of your mind like a busy train station. Thoughts are just trains pulling in and out—some bring welcome visitors, while others carry passengers you'd rather not meet. But you're not required to board every train that arrives. You can stand on the platform, notice what's passing through, and choose which ones deserve your attention.

Your brain generates thousands of thoughts every day—most of them repetitive, many of them untrue. The voice that tells you you're not enough, not capable, or not worthy is just old programming running in the background. It's not your truth. It's not your identity. It's just neurological noise that you've mistaken for reality.

The moment you realize you are not your thoughts—that you are the awareness *observing* your thoughts—everything shifts. You become the witness, not the victim. You gain the power to ask the question: *Is this thought helpful? Is it true? Does believing this serve me or limit me?*

THE INVISIBLE WINS

Your body has "archived" pain. But it can also "archive" healing.

And healing rewrites your story the same way trauma wrote it: through repetitive, tiny efforts.

Every time you pause instead of snapping... that's a record.

Every time you take one more breath when breathing feels like work... that's a record.

Every time you ask for help when you'd rather disappear... that's a record.

You get out of bed when everything feels dark... That's a record.

These are **invisible wins**—small, quiet victories that nobody applauds, but your nervous system remembers.

They're your nervous system learning: *I am worth care. I am safe enough—right now—to take one more step.*

Transformation rarely shows up with fireworks. It shows up as a tiny shift you almost miss... until one day you realize you're carrying the weight differently.

In the next chapter, I'll show you how tiny steps become the most strategic way to rebuild—because they work with your brain's wiring, not against it.

BRAIN NOTES: HOW STRESS LIVES ON

Your body doesn't just remember—it archives experiences with remarkable precision. Here's how this works in ways you can actually feel in your daily life:

Your Stress Response Is Personal

That knot in your stomach before a presentation? It's not just nerves—it's your body accessing its archives. If you bombed a speech in eighth grade, your body remembers and recreates similar physical sensations decades later. This isn't your imagination—it's your autonomic nervous system running the same program it created during past stress.

> **Try This**: Next time you feel anxious, place your hand where you feel it physically. Is it your chest? Stomach? Throat? This location is part of your personal stress signature. Simply noticing this pattern is the first step to changing it.

Emotional Memories Have Physical Addresses

When you smell your grandmother's perfume and suddenly feel safe, or hear a song that transports you instantly to high school, you're experiencing how emotions are stored with sensory details. The amygdala tags memories with these sensory elements, creating powerful triggers that bypass conscious thought.

Try This: Create a "sensory anchor" by pairing a specific scent (like lavender oil) with moments of calm. Eventually, just smelling that scent can trigger your body's relaxation response.

Your Cells Are Constantly Listening

The stress hormone cortisol doesn't just affect your mood—it alters how your genes express themselves. When chronically elevated, it can turn on genes associated with inflammation and turn off genes that help with immune function. This is why chronic stress is linked to everything from heart disease to digestive problems.

Try This: Even three deep breaths can shift your body from stress mode to rest mode, changing the chemical messages your cells receive. It sounds too simple to work, but the research is clear—breathing patterns directly impact gene expression.

Your Nervous System Can Be Retrained

Your autonomic nervous system has two main branches: the sympathetic and parasympathetic. Trauma can keep your sympathetic system stuck "on," reinforcing feelings of stress, but specific practices can strengthen your parasympathetic response.

Try This: The vagus nerve is your body's natural brake pedal for stress. Stimulate it by humming, singing, or gargling for 30 seconds. You'll feel a subtle shift as your body moves from alert to calm. This is neuroplasticity in action, and you can feel it working in real time.

The most empowering aspect of how your body archives experience is that the same mechanisms that store trauma can be used to encode healing. Every time you create a moment of safety, connection, or joy, you're writing new information into your archives, one tiny experience at a time.

CHAPTER 4
THE POWER OF TINY STEPS

WHEN EVERYONE THINKS YOU'RE FINE (BUT YOU'RE BARELY SURVIVING)

"The journey of a thousand miles begins with a single step."— Lao Tzu

In the quote above, Lao Tzu wasn't simply imparting philosophical wisdom in ancient China. This sixth-century BCE philosopher understood something profound about human transformation that modern neuroscience is only now confirming with brain scans and clinical studies. His wisdom wasn't just poetic —it was predictive of how our brains actually work.

When you're carrying the weight of trauma or chronic stress, even the smallest tasks can feel monumental. Getting out of bed, taking a shower, making a phone call—these aren't just items on a to-do list; they're mountains to climb when your brain's control panel is completely malfunctioning.

The world sees you functioning and assumes you're fine, but many don't recognize the enormous effort it takes to appear normal when your nervous system is screaming. They don't understand that you're not thriving—you're surviving—and the quality of your life is slowly suffocating under this invisible weight.

This is why tiny steps matter so much. When the weight is crushing, you don't need someone telling you to run a marathon. You need permission to celebrate taking a single step.

WHEN TRAUMA HIJACKS YOUR BRAIN'S CONTROL ROOM

Think of your brain like a high-end sound mixing board—not the simple ones at karaoke bars, but the massive professional consoles with hundreds of knobs and sliders used by sound engineers.

Your brain has its own control panel with several critical dials, including one that controls cortisol. This stress hormone isn't just released when facing a tiger; it's pumped out every morning to help you face the day. And when trauma hits, this dial gets stuck on maximum.

Then there's the memory knob, managed by your hippocampus. This seahorse-shaped structure isn't just storing random information. It's filing away episodic memories, specific events tied to times and places. This was the focus of my PhD research, studying how this structure changes in different types of dementia. When this knob malfunctions, you might remember the face of your childhood bully with perfect clarity but forget where you put your keys five minutes before.

The emotional fader regulates your feelings, while the focus switch —what neuroscientists call the Reticular Activating System—directs your attention like a spotlight.

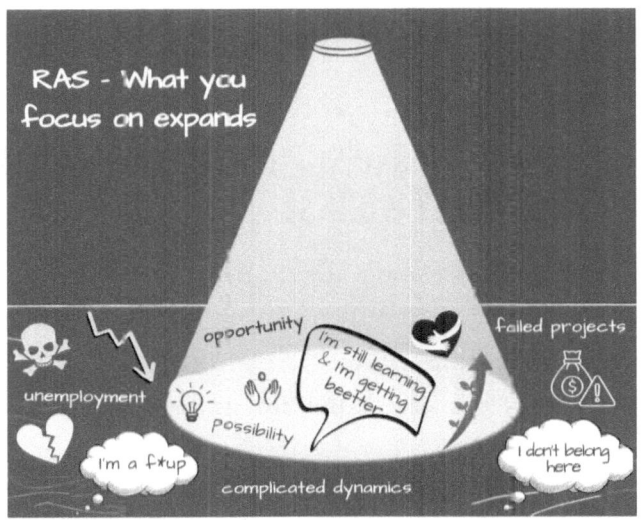

Have you ever noticed that in a crowded, noisy restaurant, the moment someone at another table says your name, your ears perk up? That's your RAS filtering out everything except what matters to you.

Or think about when you're job hunting. Suddenly, every LinkedIn post, every conversation, and every news article seems to mention career opportunities, while your friend scrolling their feed sees recipes and vacation photos.

Same content, different RAS settings.

Why does this matter for your healing? When trauma rewires your RAS, it becomes hypervigilant—constantly scanning for threats and replaying painful memories, filtering for everything that confirms you're not safe. But just as your RAS learned to focus on danger, you can retrain it to notice safety, progress, and tiny wins.

After trauma, these controls get stuck. But you can learn to be your own sound engineer.

WHY YOUR NEW YEAR'S RESOLUTIONS KEEP FAILING (AND WHAT ACTUALLY WORKS)

Here's where it gets interesting. Recent neural imaging studies show that mindfulness practice can increase gray matter in the prefrontal cortex, which is responsible for rational thinking and decision-making. It reduces the size of the amygdala—your fear center. It strengthens connections in the hippocampus—your memory center.

This means every tiny positive action you take has the ability to literally reshape your brain's architecture. You're not just changing your habits—you're changing your brain.

But if our brains are so flexible, why do New Year's resolutions fail? Because we're fighting against 86 billion neurons that have spent years wiring themselves into patterns. Your brain has created super-highways for your current habits: scrolling through your phone, reaching for comfort food, and avoiding difficult conversations. These neural pathways are so well-worn that your brain can execute them on autopilot.

When you try to force a massive change overnight, you're asking your brain to bulldoze those superhighways and build entirely new roads. It's exhausting. It requires constant willpower. And willpower, as research shows, is a limited resource.

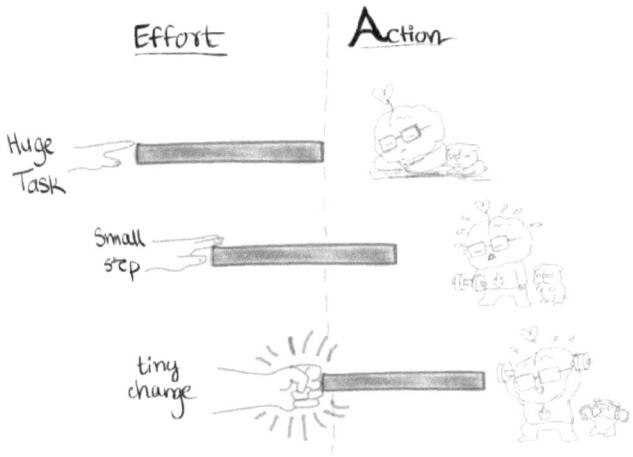

Here's what actually works: **tiny habits**.

Stanford scientist B.J. Fogg spent decades studying behavior change and wrote the book *Tiny Habits*. His formula is elegantly simple:

Prompt + Ability + Motivation → Behavior

When you set a huge goal like "meditate 20 minutes daily," you need high motivation every single day. But motivation fluctuates. Some days you're fired up. Other days, you can barely get out of bed.

Tiny habits work because they don't rely on motivation. They're so small that your ability to do them is always high.

- Instead of "meditate 20 minutes," try "take three deep breaths after my morning coffee."
- Instead of "exercise five times a week," try "do two push-ups after I brush my teeth."
- Instead of "journal every night," try "write one sentence on how one thing did not go wrong today."

These actions are so small they slip past your brain's resistance. Your basal ganglia *(habit circuitry)* doesn't sound the alarm because there's no threat. And here's the magic Fogg discovered: **You have to celebrate immediately after.**

Not later. Not when you've done it for 30 days straight. *Right now.*

After those three deep breaths? Say "Yes!" or do a little fist pump or smile and think, "I did it."

After those two push-ups? Give yourself a mental high-five.

After that one sentence? Feel proud for three seconds.

Why does this matter? **Small actions create small wins. Celebrating those small wins triggers dopamine. Dopamine reinforces the behavior.**

This is the dopamine feedback loop—the same mechanism that makes scrolling social media addictive, but now working *for* you instead of against you.

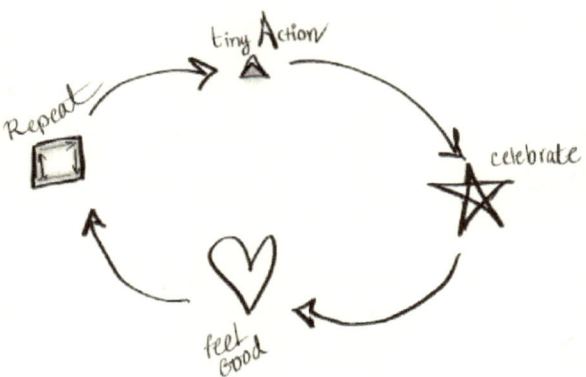

Neurons that fire together, wire together. Each tiny habit creates a new neural pathway. Each celebration strengthens it. The more you repeat it, the stronger that pathway becomes. Eventually, it becomes automatic—wired into your basal ganglia's habit circuitry.

You're not relying on willpower anymore. You're building new wiring.

And no one understood this better than a woman who was told she'd never be able to learn at all.

THE WOMAN WHO PROVED "IMPOSSIBLE" IS JUST AN OPINION

Let me tell you about Temple Grandin. Born in 1947, she entered a world that had no framework for understanding autism. Doctors told her mother to institutionalize her, to give up on her future. Why? Because Temple experienced the world as an overwhelming assault of sensations. Her brain interprets and processes things differently.

For Temple, every sound wasn't just loud. It was a thunderclap directly in her ear. Every touch wasn't just contact. It was an electric shock on her skin. Imagine living in a world where the hum of fluorescent lights feels like someone screaming directly into your brain, where the tag on your shirt feels like sandpaper rubbing your neck raw.

What makes Temple's story so relevant isn't just that she overcame these challenges; it's *how* she did it. Instead of trying to rewire her brain completely in one massive overhaul (which would have failed), she and her mother understood something profound about tiny adjustments.

Instead of forcing eye contact (which was physically painful for her), she learned to glance briefly. Rather than fighting her need for pressure (which calmed her nervous system), she invented a "squeeze machine" that provided deep pressure without human touch. Instead of broad changes, she made micro-adjustments to her environment that allowed her brain to process information differently.

Today, Temple Grandin holds a PhD. She is a professor, author, and one of the most influential voices in both autism advocacy and animal science. Her story isn't about "overcoming" her brain. It's about understanding how it works and building tiny systems that work *with* it.

Temple didn't wake up one day and force herself to be "normal." She took small steps—one sensory accommodation, one visual thinking strategy, one design at a time.

She proved that different doesn't mean broken and that tiny, consistent steps can lead to extraordinary impact. This is what I mean by **mindfulness in work boots**—practical, tangible actions that meet your brain where it is.

Temple's story shows us what's possible when we work with our brain's unique wiring—but what happens when the brain loses its ability to remember anything at all?

THE MAN WHO FORGOT EVERYTHING BUT NEVER LOST JOY

There's a famous gentleman on TikTok named Mr. Gene who has dementia, which means his memory resets every 15 minutes or so.

More often than not, he can't remember what he had for breakfast or who he spoke with last.

Yet every day when the school bus arrives, like clockwork, Mr. Gene goes to sit outside. Even though his conscious memory is damaged, something deeper drives him.

While our cognitive memories live in the hippocampus, our emotional memories and habits are stored throughout our brain and body. Even when the hippocampus is damaged, other brain structures maintain these procedural memories, the unconscious knowledge of how to do things.

Every day, stepping off the bus, children jump off to greet him, reintroducing themselves as if they're meeting for the first time. And even though he can't remember their names or faces, his face lights up with pure joy. His body remembers the happiness from these interactions, even when his mind cannot hold the details.

This shows us something profound:

- Joy can create pathways that survive even when memory fails.
- Tiny consistent actions build powerful patterns.
- Our bodies can remember what our minds forget.
- Connection leaves imprints deeper than conscious thought.

Think about what this means for healing from trauma. Just as Mr. Gene's brain found a way to guide him to joy despite severe memory loss, our brains can create new pathways to safety and connection, even when past trauma has rewired our threat detection system.

THE POWER OF INVISIBLE WINS

You don't have to fix everything at once. You just need to find the one small adjustment that makes the next step possible.

Here's what I've learned from Temple Grandin's micro-adjustments, from Mr. Gene's daily routine, from the neuroscience of tiny habits, and from my own journey through trauma: the most powerful changes happen in the moments no one else sees.

This is why I founded Invisible Wins LLC—not just as a company, but as a movement. A movement for all the invisible winners who fight quiet battles that no one sees, who wake up, show up, and do the work that no one applauds.

Through my work, I aim to honor the voiceless.

Invisible wins are the quiet, everyday victories that often go unnoticed by others but are deeply meaningful to us. They are the small acts of courage, self-care, and resilience that help us move forward, even when no one else sees.

Invisible wins look like:

- Getting out of bed on a hard day
- Saying "no" when you need to
- Taking a mindful breath
- Reaching out for support

But they also look like brushing your teeth when suicidal thoughts are circling. They look like they're choosing to eat something nourishing instead of numbing the pain. They look like answering your phone when your nervous system is screaming that everyone is judging you. They look like they're making lunch for your kids while your anxiety whispers that you're failing at everything.

Invisible winners are the people who keep going, even when their progress isn't visible to the world. They show up for themselves and others in small, powerful ways—choosing self-compassion, setting boundaries, and celebrating their own quiet victories.

Invisible winners remind us that true strength is often found in the moments no one else sees.

Your invisible wins are the building blocks of recovery. They're proof that even when your brain's control panel is hijacked, even when trauma has rewired your threat detection system, you still have agency. You still have power.

The world celebrates the obvious victories—the promotions, the marathons, the dramatic before-and-after transformations. But we're here to celebrate the invisible ones—the tiny, brave acts that are literally rewiring your brain toward healing.

You are an invisible winner. Your quiet battles matter. Your small steps count. Your courage to keep trying, even when no one is watching, is changing the world, one tiny win at a time.

YOUR JOURNEY STARTS RIGHT HERE

Just as trauma can hijack your brain circuitry, you can learn to rewire it. Just as negative thoughts can become automatic, you can build new neuronal pathways to hope.

It's not just what people say to you—it's your relationship with your own thoughts. Remember, thoughts themselves are neutral. They're electrical impulses firing across synapses. It's the meaning we assign to them and the stories we tell about them that create suffering.

The question isn't whether you can change; it's whether or not you're ready to think differently.

Let's rewire our brains together, one tiny step at a time.

BRAIN NOTES: THE NEUROSCIENCE OF TINY HABITS

Your brain is literally built to benefit from tiny steps, not massive overhauls. Here's why small changes work so powerfully in your everyday life:

Your Habit Superhighway

Every time you repeat an action, you're paving a neural pathway. Do it enough, and you create what neuroscientists call "long-term potentiation," which you can think of as a superhighway in your brain that automates your behavior. This is why you can drive home without thinking about the route or brush your teeth while half-asleep.

> **Try This**: To build a new habit, stack it onto an existing one. Want to remember vitamins? Put them by your coffee maker. Your brain's existing coffee routine becomes the on-ramp to your new vitamin habit.

The Motivation Molecule

Dopamine isn't just about pleasure—it's about anticipation and motivation. When you complete even a tiny task successfully, your brain releases dopamine, which doesn't just make you feel good—it makes you want to repeat the behavior.

> **Try This**: Break down any challenging task into ridiculously

small steps. Instead of "exercise daily," try "put on my workout shoes." Your brain's reward system activates even for this tiny win, creating momentum for the next step.

The Threat-Detection Bypass

Your amygdala treats big changes as potential threats, triggering resistance while allowing tiny habits to fly under its radar. When you make changes so small they don't trigger fear, you bypass the brain's natural resistance to change.

> **Try This**: If meditation for ten minutes feels overwhelming, start with just one mindful breath. Your brain won't sound the alarm for something this small, allowing you to establish the practice without resistance.

The Compound Effect in Action

Your brain doesn't distinguish between physical and mental training—both create structural changes through a process called neuroplasticity. Just as compound interest transforms small financial investments over time, tiny consistent actions create compound growth in neural pathways.

> **Try this:** Track your tiny wins in a visible way. Each check-mark on a calendar or note in your phone creates visual proof of your progress, reinforcing the neural pathways you're building.

The Willpower Conservation Method

Your prefrontal cortex, responsible for decision-making and willpower, has limited energy. Making decisions depletes this resource in a process called "ego depletion." Tiny habits require minimal decision-making energy, making them sustainable even when willpower is low.

> **Try This**: Prepare your environment in advance to make tiny habits automatic. Put your workout clothes next to your bed, prepare healthy snacks at eye level in your fridge, or set digital reminders that make good choices the path of least resistance.

The most powerful aspect of tiny habits isn't just that they're easier to start—it's that they work with your brain's natural wiring rather than against it. Every small step you take isn't just changing your behavior—it's physically rewiring your brain's architecture, one tiny neural connection at a time.

PART THREE
THINK FRAMEWORK

CHAPTER 5
LETTER "T" – TRACK THE NEGATIVE THOUGHTS

CATCH THE LOOP BEFORE IT CATCHES YOU

What derails us most often isn't the big, obvious crisis—it's the mental routines we run on autopilot. Have you ever noticed how a single negative comment can echo in your mind for days, while 10 compliments evaporate instantly? That's not your imagination. It's your brain's ancient survival system at work.

The most dangerous patterns in your life are the ones you never notice, the silent thought loops running in the background while you're just trying to get through the day. For a long time, I treated every thought as a command instead of a suggestion, until I started examining them the way an engineer troubleshoots a system: step back, observe, test.

7 WORDS THAT SHATTERED MY WORLD

Earlier in the book, 7 words held the power to change everything following my assault: "We have more important cases to handle."

After months of waiting for justice, the detective's dismissal hit like a tsunami. In that moment, I felt erased. Invisible.

As a neuroscientist, I understood that my brain's threat response was in overdrive. But when you're in that dark place, what you know intellectually goes straight out the window—knowledge isn't enough to stop the spiral.

I was paralyzed, stuck in a loop of toxic thoughts:

- *I'm not important enough.*
- *Why even try?*
- *Nobody cares.*

Maybe your trigger isn't a dismissive detective. Maybe it's an email from your boss that keeps you awake at night, or a casual comment from a family member that constantly repeats in your mind.

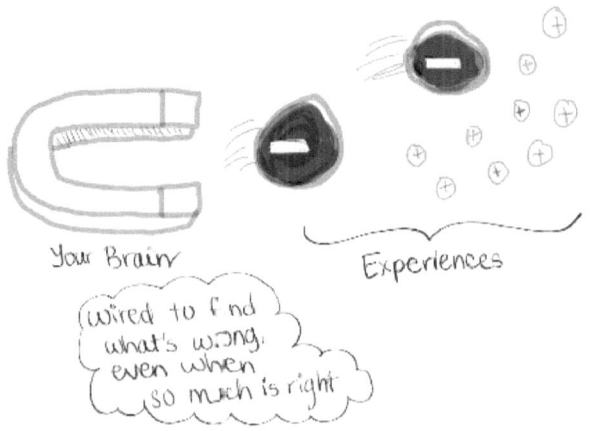

Your Brain

Experiences

(wired to find what's wrong, even when so much is right)

We've all been there, caught in the undertow of our thoughts, powerless to swim back to shore.

YOUR BRAIN'S HIDDEN TAX SYSTEM

Your brain generates about 60,000 thoughts per day.

Think of your mind as Times Square on New Year's Eve, constantly buzzing with activity, flashing lights, and messages competing for attention. But here's the kicker: ~80 percent of these thoughts are negative, with 95 percent repeating from yesterday, last week, or years ago.

My boss telling me I should "do better" five years ago still triggers anxiety during every evaluation. These aren't even fresh thoughts—they're old wounds reopening.

Like having too many apps open on your phone, these repeated negative thoughts quietly drain your mental battery. You have finite resources. When that battery is getting sucked by old loops, there's less energy left for what matters now: your work, your relationships, your creativity, and your joy.

THE THREE INVISIBLE TRAPS STEALING YOUR LIFE

Through my journey, I've discovered three hidden traps that keep us stuck on mental autopilot:

1. The Distorted Lens

Think of this as a filter on your camera lens that warps every photo you take. Our past experiences create invisible biases that color how we see every situation.

After my assault, I viewed every social gathering through a lens of potential exclusion and threat. Maybe for you, when you see that certain coworker, you close up without knowing why—perhaps it's their nonverbal cues triggering something from your past.

2. The Dangerous Shortcuts

Our brains create neuronal shortcuts based on past experiences. Efficient for driving your regular route to work, but brutal when the shortcut is:

Social gathering = potential dismissal and exclusion = retreat to safety.

For years, I followed that script without realizing it.

3. The Mental Traffic Jam

With 60,000 daily thoughts competing for attention, our brains get overwhelmed. The noise drowns out the important signals, much like trying to hear your friend in Times Square on New Year's Eve.

THE DEBT I DIDN'T KNOW I WAS PAYING

After the assault, I tried to keep busy by bartending. On the surface, I was functioning. Underneath, my mind was jammed.

What most people didn't see was how hard it was to talk to friends who didn't understand what I'd been through or who avoided the subject because it felt too heavy. I was also finishing my PhD, writing a thesis on Alzheimer's disease, work I cared deeply about. But my mental resources were running on empty.

I hadn't been processing my emotional trash. I'd been storing it. It piled up in the corners of my mind until the whole place started to stink.

So while everyone else in my program moved forward—attending events, laughing together, supporting each other—I sat alone, feeling invisible. Every time they mentioned shared experiences, my reaction wasn't about them. It was about that phone call from the detective. About the night everything changed.

Years later, the same pattern showed up with my partner's friends. I'd retreat and then blame him for not standing up for me, and we'd fight. Only much later did I realize those fights weren't really about dinner plans—they were about a deeper wound that had never been named.

That's what happens when we're not aware of our thoughts. The cost compounds quietly until it feels like your mind is going bankrupt.

THE EMPEROR WHO MASTERED HIS MIND DURING CHAOS

Two thousand years ago, during one of history's most chaotic periods, a remarkable man practiced what neuroscientists now confirm as one of the most powerful tools for mental mastery.

Marcus Aurelius wasn't born to be emperor. Orphaned young and unexpectedly adopted into the imperial family, he found himself ruling Rome (161–180 AD) during a time of plagues that killed millions, constant wars on multiple borders, and political betrayal, including from his own co-emperor.

Yet amid this chaos, Marcus did something extraordinary. Each night, he wrote in his journals, tracking his thoughts and examining his reactions to the day's events. These writings, later published as *Meditations*, weren't meant for anyone else to read—they were his way of monitoring his mind.

"The happiness of your life depends upon the quality of your thoughts," he wrote. *"When you arise in the morning, think of what a precious privilege it is to be alive—to breathe, to think, to enjoy, to love."*

If a man running an empire in crisis could carve out time to examine his own thoughts, maybe we can find a minute to look at ours. Marcus wasn't a monk in a peaceful monastery—he was a leader facing daily disasters, yet he still prioritized mental awareness.

Modern neuroscience confirms what this ancient leader intuited: the simple act of observing our thoughts literally rewires our brain.

THE SILENT GIRL WHO FOUND HER VOICE

Another powerful example comes from a woman whose early trauma could have defined her life but instead became the foundation for her greatness.

Maya Angelou, born in 1928 during the harsh reality of racial segregation in America, experienced sexual abuse at age seven. After she identified her abuser, the man was killed, likely by her uncles. Believing her voice had caused his death, Maya went mute for almost five years.

During this period of silence, something remarkable happened. Unable to speak, Maya developed an extraordinary awareness of her thoughts and the world around her. She absorbed thousands of books, memorized poetry, and observed human behavior with unusual depth.

Later, in her autobiography, *I Know Why the Caged Bird Sings*, she described how this period of silence led to heightened internal awareness. As an adult, Maya also used writing as a form of tracking thoughts, often renting hotel rooms as a place to document and examine her inner world.

"There is no greater agony than bearing an untold story inside you," she wrote.

Both Marcus and Maya, separated by centuries and circumstances, discovered the same truth: awareness of our thoughts is the first step toward freedom from them.

THE SCIENCE OF TAKING BACK CONTROL

We can't always choose our circumstances. We can choose how we train our brains to respond.

Dr. Lisa Feldman Barrett's research shows that our default mode network—our brain's autopilot—is most active when our mind is wandering. That's one reason people stay busy: when you're focused on a task, you can't ruminate as easily. But when you start tracking your thoughts, you engage your prefrontal cortex—the part of your brain involved in planning and self-control—and take the wheel back from autopilot.

Studies from MIT show that people who spend just 15 minutes a day monitoring their thoughts improve emotional regulation by about 32 percent in eight weeks. Dr. Caroline Leaf's work suggests consistent thought tracking can reduce negative thinking by around 62 percent over two months.

Even your genes respond. These mental practices affect our epigenetics. While your DNA sequence doesn't change, your experiences and mental habits can influence how genes turn "on" or "off." Same hardware, upgraded software.

YOUR INVISIBLE WIN STARTS WITH AWARENESS

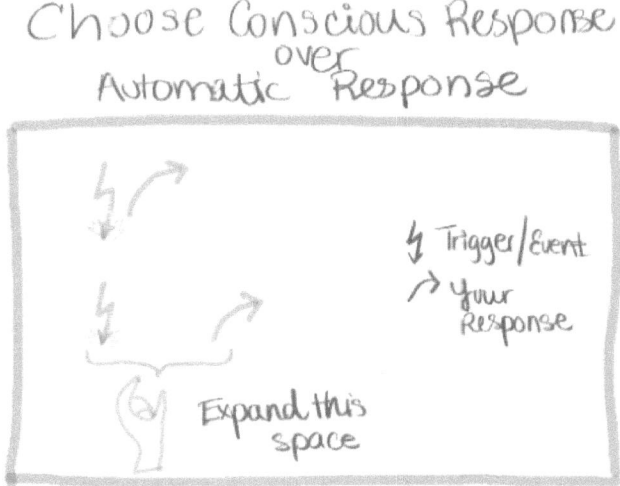

Tracking your thoughts is like installing a security camera in your mind. You finally see who keeps sneaking in and what they're stealing.

When I began noticing how I felt with certain people and in specific situations, I could make small, proactive changes instead of living on autopilot. That's how this framework started: with tracking. It wasn't quick. It took years to move from paralysis to power. But the brain structures I used are the same ones you have. We all have the capacity to rewire our thinking.

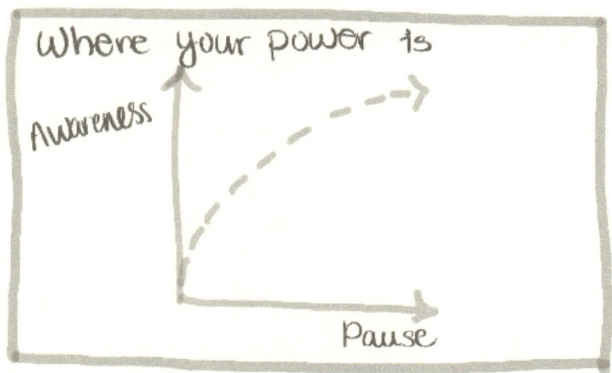

SMALL STEPS, MASSIVE FREEDOM

You don't have to track 60,000 thoughts. It is overwhelmingly impossible. Start with one minute a day. Think of yourself as a scientist studying the most fascinating subject in the world, your own mind.

Here are two simple techniques I teach my clients:

1. **The Screenshot Method**: A few times a day, pause and ask, *What am I thinking right now?* Take a mental screenshot. Over time, you'll start seeing patterns.
2. **The Timestamp Technique**: Notice **when** certain thoughts show up. What do you think right before a big meeting? Around certain family members? In social gatherings?

Remember that you are not your thoughts. You are not what other people say about you. You are the awareness behind them.

We will always feel powerless if we let our minds wander aimlessly. So take back control. As a neuroscientist, coach, and fellow traveler on this journey called life (with all its shitty experiences), I promise you, this is just the beginning of your brain's remarkable story.

I can't tell you when things will get better or when you'll conquer negative thoughts completely. But I know your remarkable story starts with being aware and tracking your own thoughts.

Your invisible win begins today.

Track Your Thoughts

Recap:

- Your brain generates approximately 60,000 thoughts daily, with 80 percent of them negative and 95 percent repeating from previous days.
- Negativity bias is an evolutionary adaptation that helped our ancestors survive by prioritizing threats.
- The default mode network activates when we're not consciously directing our thoughts, often leading to rumination.
- Tracking thoughts activates the prefrontal cortex, strengthening cognitive control.

- Epigenetics shows that mental practices can change how genes express themselves without changing your DNA.
- Just 15 minutes of daily thought tracking can improve emotional regulation by 32 percent in eight weeks.
- Consistent thought awareness can reduce negative thinking by 62 percent over two months.
- The brain creates neuronal shortcuts based on past experiences, which can lead to automatic negative reactions.
- Awareness itself changes brain activity patterns, shifting from the emotional amygdala to the rational prefrontal cortex.

BRAIN NOTES: THE SCIENCE OF THOUGHT AWARENESS

Your Brain's Default Setting

When you're not focused on a specific task, your brain's default mode network activates, often replaying negative thoughts and memories. This isn't a design flaw—it's your brain's way of scanning for potential threats. Brain imaging studies show this network consumes up to 20 percent of your body's energy, explaining why rumination feels so exhausting.

> **Try This:** Set a gentle alarm for three random times throughout your day. When it sounds, simply notice what you were thinking about. Don't judge or change your thoughts—just observe them. This tiny practice activates your prefrontal cortex, shifting activity away from the default mode network.

The Negativity Bias in Action

Your brain gives roughly three times more attention to negative experiences than positive ones. This evolutionary adaptation helped our ancestors survive by prioritizing potential threats. Today, this means a single criticism often outweighs multiple compliments in your mental accounting system.

> **Try This:** Before bed, write down three positive moments from your day, no matter how small. This simple practice

counterbalances your brain's negativity bias and, when done consistently, strengthens neural pathways that notice positive experiences.

Thought Patterns and Neural Highways

Every thought you think travels along neural pathways in your brain. Repeated thoughts—whether positive or negative—strengthen these pathways through a process called long-term potentiation. This is why habitual thought patterns become automatic and increasingly difficult to change over time.

> **Try This:** Choose one recurring negative thought. Create a specific "if-then" plan: *If I notice myself thinking [negative thought], then I will take one deep breath.* This tiny interruption creates a moment of awareness that weakens the automatic neural pathway.

The Observer Effect in Your Brain

The simple act of observing your thoughts activates your prefrontal cortex. When this region engages, it can regulate the emotional reactivity of your amygdala, explaining why awareness, without any attempt to change your thoughts, can reduce their emotional impact by up to 30 percent.

> **Try this:** Practice the "name it to tame it" technique. When a strong emotion arises, simply label it: *"This is anxiety"* or *"This is frustration."* This tiny linguistic act creates distance between you and the emotion, reducing amygdala activation within seconds.

Your Thoughts and Your Genes

Your thought patterns influence how your genes express themselves through epigenetics. Chronic stress and negative rumination can activate genes associated with inflammation, while mindfulness practices can activate genes associated with improved immune function—all without changing your DNA sequence.

> **Try this:** Set a tiny daily reminder to take three mindful breaths. Research shows that even this micro-practice, when done consistently, can create measurable changes in gene expression related to stress response within just eight weeks.

CHAPTER 6

LETTER "H" – HALT
NEGATIVE PATTERNS

WHEN TOXIC MOLD MEETS TOXIC THOUGHTS

Eight months into my job search, when my mind and body were already exhausted, our tiny New York studio turned on us.

One evening, I noticed the kitchen wallpaper peeling. When we finally pulled it back, we discovered patches of dark mold spreading across the wall—tiny spores we'd been inhaling every day. I'm allergic to mold, so my body went into full alarm: dizziness, tight chest, burning lungs. Our dog, Iri, started getting sick, too.

Our home, the one place that was supposed to feel safe, had become another threat.

You'll hear more about that mold in the next chapter. For now, what matters is **when** it hits: right on top of unemployment, financial stress, and a mountain of rejection. It didn't just add a new problem. It amplified every old story my brain was already playing on repeat.

THE SPIRAL BEFORE THE STORM

Let's rewind eight months.

I had just finished my PhD in neuroscience. After the trauma I'd endured, I knew I didn't want to stay in academia. I needed something different. So I took a leap, learned to code, and started aiming for data science.

Which meant I was unemployed.

While my fellow graduates stepped into prestigious postdocs and industry jobs, I was at home, teaching myself Python and SQL from scratch. My mom called constantly.

"What are you going to do with your PhD? Why are you trying something completely different after wasting so many years?"

She couldn't see that I was suffocating from what psychologists call "negative familiarity"—when painful, unhealthy patterns feel like home because they're what you know.

During this time, I was deeply grateful to my sister and partner, who agreed that the three of us would live together to save on rent. I contributed what little I could from my savings as I built new skills.

Finally, I landed an amazing job at a mission-driven medical startup. The work was meaningful. The people were brilliant. For the first time in a long while, there was hope in my chest again.

Then the funding dried up.

I was laid off.

THE MOUNTAIN OF REJECTION

I had transitioned from dreaming about improving people's lives and their brains through my research to dealing with the aftermath of sexual assault, finishing my PhD, starting over, learning how to code, and finally getting my dream job before I lost it.

"Whiplash" was the only word for it.

At first, I stayed positive. *Come on, Khai,* I told myself. *You have a PhD and coding skills now. Finding a job should be a breeze!*

I customized countless resumes and cover letters. I studied nights and weekends. Days turned into weeks, then months, with nothing to show for it.

In the tech industry, each job interview is like climbing Mount Everest. I had to go through multiple rounds: phone screening with recruiters, phone interviews with hiring managers, technical assessments, take-home assignments, and finally, if you're lucky, an on-site interview with the hiring manager and the rest of the team, where they grilled you as if you were in an interrogation room. It could be *that* intimidating. And after all of that? A soul-crushing email beginning with, *"We're sorry to inform you that you're not a good fit."*

I stopped counting after 4,046 rejections. At some point, the rejections became a story I told myself about who I was. Still, I continued to refresh my inbox like a scoreboard I couldn't win.

I found myself caught in a negative spiral, questioning the point of opening emails or applying for more jobs.

And then, eight months into my job search nightmare, I found myself in a moldy studio, unemployed, inhaling toxicity, and battling a body I couldn't control. It was the perfect storm.

God, WTF is this? I'm so tired. Just... tired. Every time I think I'm through something, there's more waiting. And I know—maybe I'm supposed to grow from this, maybe it means something. If I'm supposed to matter, if this is supposed to lead somewhere... I actually need to survive it. And I don't know if I will.

WHEN YOUR BRAIN WORKS AGAINST YOU

Remember the negativity bias we discussed in Chapter 5? Our brains are wired to focus on the negative, to notice what's wrong first. At the time, all I could see were repeated patterns of rejection everywhere I looked—every application submitted, every email received.

Research indicates that negative experiences have a greater impact on us than positive ones. The shame of being jobless with a fancy degree for eight months was overwhelming. I wasn't just sitting on the couch watching Netflix—I was trying everything I could think of, but nothing worked.

As a neuroscientist, I again understood what was happening. These rejection emails had become mental quicksand, each one pulling me deeper into thoughts of *I'm not good enough.*

When we encounter a trigger like a rejection email, our amygdala activates within 74 milliseconds—faster than we can consciously process the word "no"—often leaving our rational brain no time to weigh in before the body floods with stress signals and stress hormones, including cortisol.

The inner voices get loud fast: *"You're not enough. You're failing. You'll never catch up."* How often do you replay negative voices in your head? Whose voices are they? Your own? Your parents? Others who said you'd never succeed?

These voices are what keep us trapped in negative patterns.

BREAKING FREE: THE POWER OF PATTERN INTERRUPTION

So how do you fight a system that moves before you think? You get proactive and interrupt it.

When we consciously break negative thought patterns, we create what neuroscientists refer to as a "pattern interruption," a brief action (two-to three-second window) that creates a pause between trigger and reaction.

This pause allows your brain's "gear shift," the anterior cingulate cortex, and your prefrontal cortex to take the wheel. Sometimes, the pause is physical: standing up from a chair, shaking out your arms, or taking a short walk to the window. Sometimes, it's sensory: splashing cool water on your wrists, stepping into a different room, holding a cold glass. Sometimes, it's a deliberate shift in how you're thinking about that moment (the story, labels, or questions in your head) that creates a pause between trigger and reaction. Instead of moving your body (physical) or changing your sensations (sensory), you change the meaning you're giving the situation on purpose.

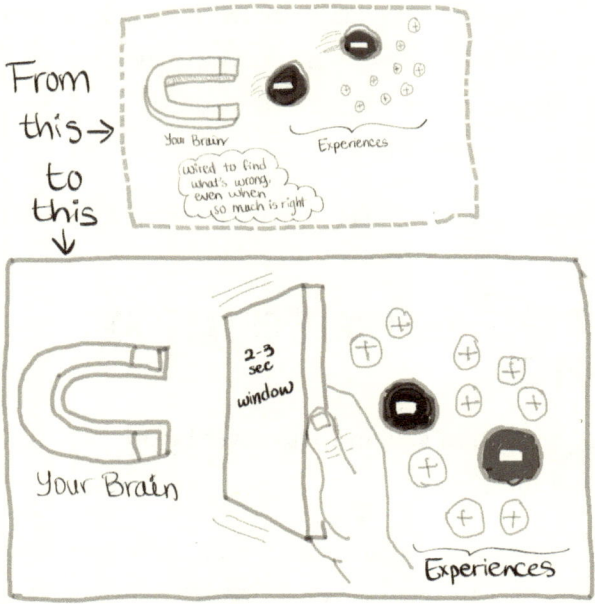

Here's one way you can proactively change the story in your head:

1. Name what you feel.
2. Then, ask a better question that moves you forward.

Name it: "I feel anger in my jaw because that comment stung."

Reframe with a question:

- "What's my next smallest step?"
- "What else could be true besides 'I suck'?"
- "What part of this is in my control for the next 10 minutes?"

Ground it:

- "Fact: it's one rejection, not my identity."
- "I can reply tomorrow. Tonight I am choosing to step away."

Make it visible: write your favorite question or grounding line on a sticky note (or your phone lock screen) and put it where you'll see it —laptop cover, wallet, bathroom mirror. When the spiral starts, glance at it and run your two-step: name it, then ask a better question. That tiny pause lets your "gear shift" and prefrontal cortex take the wheel.

When we're spiraling downward, it can feel impossible to climb back up. Advice we often hear against sending angry emails is proven by biology. Taking a step back enables your amygdala to calm down and your rational mind to reactivate.

After being jobless for eight months, it would have been easy to stop trying. Negative thought patterns kept popping up in my head, but I knew I needed to interrupt them. Nine months in, I finally found myself a mentor, someone in the industry who could guide me. Coincidentally, at the time, I was in the late phase of the interview process with a prestigious bank for a data scientist position—I passed the phone interview, the technical discussion with the hiring manager, and the take-home assessment. Next was the on-site interview.

With my mentor beside me, I was confident. But as we prepared one day, you'd never guess what he told me: "You are not ready."

Talk about triggering my negativity bias again! My first thought was, *"See, Khai? You're a failure. You'll never be good enough. You're just dumb. If my own mentor doesn't believe in me, how can I believe in myself?"*

Maybe you've felt that punch. Maybe it wasn't a mentor but a boss who was supposed to have your back but didn't. Perhaps your parents, who were supposed to protect you, instead caused you emotional pain.

It's no wonder we sometimes feel so messed up.

In the end, I still went to the on-site interview, though I didn't get the job. Despite my efforts to halt them, my mentor's words played in the background of my mind.

That's why learning to believe in your capacity and your uniqueness is not fluff—it's survival. When the voices come, your job isn't to silence them forever but to build a fast gear shift.

LEARNING FROM HISTORY'S PATTERN INTERRUPTERS

Nelson Mandela provides a powerful example of halting negative patterns. During his 27 years of imprisonment, he chose to stop the natural responses of hatred and bitterness. He famously said, *"As I walked out the door toward the gate that would lead to my freedom, I knew if I didn't leave my bitterness and hatred behind, I would still be in prison."* Nelson Mandela wasn't talking about physical confinement anymore, but the mental prison that negative thoughts create. Later, as president of South Africa, he backed the Truth and Reconciliation Commission—a structured way for people to face brutal facts, tell the truth, and choose a future that wasn't fueled by revenge. That is a collective pattern interruption.

Admiral James Stockdale interrupted both false optimism and despair. A U.S. Navy pilot shot down over North Vietnam, he endured more than seven years of captivity and torture, later teaching fellow POWs a mindset that would be known as the Stockdale Paradox. He wrote, *"You must not confuse faith that you will prevail in the end—which you can never afford to lose—with the discipline to confront the most brutal facts of your current reality, whatever they might be."*

The core lesson is this: hold two things at once—confront the most brutal facts of your current reality, but keep unwavering faith that you will prevail in the end. That "both/and" stance breaks two unhelpful loops—wishful thinking and hopelessness—and makes room for disciplined action.

Harriet Tubman offers another remarkable example. Instead of accepting the common belief that escape was impossible, she interrupted this thought pattern not just for herself but for others. Repeatedly, she returned by way of the Underground Railroad to guide others to freedom. She traveled at night, worked with trusted conductors, and used songs as coded signals to calm fear and keep people moving. That's pattern interruption in motion.

Different playbooks: forgiveness (Mandela), brutal honesty plus faith (Stockdale), and connection with clear signals (Tubman).

However, they all used the same through-line: create a pause, change your state, then choose the next wise step.

YOUR PERSONAL PATTERN INTERRUPTER

Pattern interruption looks different for different people. Admiral Stockdale told the truth and held the line. Harriet Tubman sang songs. You need tools that fit your life, your season, and your body. Start small.

Start by naming what you feel. Psychologists call this "affect labeling," meaning briefly putting your feelings into words. Doing this recruits control networks in your brain and can dial down amygdala activity.

Use this one-liner: "I feel [emotion] in my [body location] because [short reason]."

Examples:

"I feel tense in my neck because the feedback felt harsh."

"I feel anger in my jaw because the project got shelved."

"I feel dread in my stomach because I'm waiting on test results."

Say it out loud or type it in your notes. Name it to tame it.

Then breathe with a long exhale. One powerful pattern is "cyclic sighing":

1. Inhale through your nose.
2. Take a second short sip of air to top off.
3. Exhale slowly through your mouth.

Repeat for five to ten cycles. In a randomized study, this exhale-heavy pattern reduced daily anxiety more than a standard mindfulness practice.

If you like structure, turn it into an if-then plan (an "implementation intention"):

- *"If I get a rejection email, then I stand up, take three steps away, do five cyclic sighs, and say, 'I feel pressure in my chest because that stung.'"*
- *"If an argument starts at home, then I touch cold water, step to the doorway, and say, 'I'm heated—give me two minutes.'"*

You don't have to be perfect. You just need a plan you can execute in the wild.

Make the interruption physical when you can. The quickest way to cut through mental noise is often movement. Walk to the end of the block. Do ten push-ups against the counter. Step outside and feel the air on your face. Shake out your arms like you would before a heavy set in the gym. Motion is a message to your brain that you're shifting gears.

Here's a simple sequence you can use even in a crowded office or at the kitchen sink.

3–3–3 Halt Method

- Take 3 steps away from what you're doing.
- Take 3 deep breaths with long exhales.
- Take 3 seconds to name what you're feeling.

Each move taps a different circuit. The steps interrupt the freeze response. The breathing nudges your nervous system toward calm. The naming recruits your thinking brain. Three tiny levers, one fast state shift. You won't catch every spiral, but you'll catch more—and sooner.

For me, gospel music helps. One of my favorite songs is "Hall of Fame" by The Script. There's a lyric that says, *"You can be the King Kong bangin' on your chest,"* and I literally thump my chest when I hear it. It sounds silly, but that physical jolt breaks the loop and brings me back into my body.

Our brains are wired with negativity bias. If we don't decide how to respond when spirals come, we'll default to the old familiar patterns.

Take a moment now to imagine what an interruption might look like for you. Physical? Sensory change? A specific question you ask yourself? Tap into your creativity.

Here are some examples:

- Physical patterns: Go for a walk or run. Research shows physical movement is great for pattern interruption.
- Sensory interruption: Change your environment. During a heated conversation, move to a different part of the room or step outside.
- Cognitive redirection: Find a new focus point.

Remember: these negative patterns formed for a reason. At some point, they were trying to protect you. That's why the next step is so important: **investigating** those patterns instead of just shutting them down.

Before moving on to the next chapter, take a moment to note how you'll interrupt negative thoughts, heated conversations, or spirals when they come. You have a two- to three-second window to choose something different. Track your thoughts, notice triggers, and feel empowered to pause those automatic responses.

Halt negative Pattern

Recap:

- Your brain processes negative experiences more strongly than positive ones. The amygdala activates within 74 milliseconds of a negative trigger—faster than conscious thought.
- Breaking negative thought cycles activates your anterior cingulate cortex, creating "pattern separation" that allows new neural pathways to form.
- Practicing the 3-3-3 method engages different brain networks, reducing amygdala activity and activating your prefrontal cortex.
- Briefly labeling feelings and using exhale-heavy breathing (cyclic sighs) are fast, science-backed ways to cool the alarm and regain control.

- When you consistently interrupt negative patterns, you're physically rewiring your brain, creating new neural pathways that make positive responses more automatic over time.
- You have a two- to three-second window after recognizing a negative pattern to interrupt it before it takes over your thinking.

BRAIN NOTES: BREAKING THOUGHT LOOPS

The Amygdala's Lightning Response

The amygdala activates within 74 milliseconds after encountering a trigger—faster than conscious thought. This explains why negative thoughts can hijack your thinking before you're even aware of them.

> **Try This:** When you notice negative thoughts starting, place your hand on your chest and take one deep breath. Do 60 seconds of cyclic sighing. Inhale through your nose, take a short second sip of air, then do a long, slow exhale through your mouth. Repeat for five to ten cycles. A randomized study found this exhale-heavy pattern reduced daily anxiety more than a standard mindfulness practice. Let's give your rational brain a chance to engage.

Pattern Interruption Rewires Your Brain

When you halt a negative thought pattern, you activate your anterior cingulate cortex, or your brain's gear-shifting mechanism. This creates what neuroscientists call "pattern separation," allowing your brain to form new, healthier neural pathways.

> **Try This:** Use the 3-3-3 Method when spiraling. Take 3 steps away from where you are, take 3 deep breaths, and spend 3 seconds naming what you're feeling. This simple

sequence engages multiple brain regions, breaking the amygdala's control.

Your Two-Second Opportunity Window

Research shows you have a two- to three-second window after recognizing a negative pattern to interrupt it before it takes over. This brief moment is your chance to redirect neural activity from emotional brain centers to rational ones.

> **Try This:** Select a specific physical movement, like tapping your thumb and forefinger together, to do when you notice negative thoughts. The physical sensation creates a stronger pattern interruption than mental effort alone.

Celebration Strengthens New Neural Pathways

When you celebrate breaking negative patterns, your brain releases dopamine, which strengthens the neural pathways of your healthier response. This is why celebration is the most powerful way to wire in new habits.

> **Try This:** After successfully interrupting a negative thought, give yourself an immediate micro-celebration—a quick "Yes!" with a fist pump or smile. The smaller and quicker the celebration, the easier it is to make it consistent. Quick, frequent celebrations reinforce the habit loop.

Environment Shapes Thought Patterns

Your physical surroundings can either trigger or interrupt negative thoughts. The brain constantly scans your environment for cues that activate stored emotional responses.

Try This: When caught in a negative spiral, change your physical location—even moving to another room can help. Harvard research shows that physical movement creates one of the strongest pattern interruptions for your brain.

CHAPTER 7
LETTER "I" – INVESTIGATE THE HIDDEN PATTERNS

THAT NAGGING FEELING SOMETHING ISN'T RIGHT

Have you ever noticed something was off but couldn't quite put your finger on it? Before we found the mold, my body already knew something was wrong.

I'd wake up with headaches that felt like someone was hitting my skull with a hammer. Every breath burned. My dog threw up for three days straight. I told our building manager.

"It's all in your head," he said, rolling his eyes.

My partner felt totally fine at first, which made me question myself even more.

Maybe I am being dramatic. Maybe it is just stress.

Sure enough, though, thousands of toxic mold spores had been silently spreading through our tiny New York studio apartment, infiltrating our lungs with every breath.

Isn't it fascinating how differently our bodies respond to the same threat? The mold hit me and my dog, Iri, almost immediately. My partner didn't feel a thing for weeks. We're all wired differently, reacting to identical triggers in our own way.

The mold metaphor hit me hard later: rot hides well. So do emotional wounds.

They live behind pretty wallpaper—decent jobs, packed calendars, polite smiles. By the time you start to smell something off, it's already in your system. What lurks beneath the surface can be uncomfortable, even frightening, but only by investigating can we begin to heal.

THE HIDDEN STUFF THAT RUNS OUR LIVES

For years, I became a magician of excuses. "I have to study." "I'm too tired."

I didn't skip most of those social gatherings because I was busy; I skipped them because my nervous system was already at max volume. I'd walk in smiling, then disappear inside myself, watching conversations like a foreign film without subtitles. I felt like a ghost: in the room, but not in the circle.

And when you feel outside the circle long enough, you start keeping score—of slights, of silence, of who gets to belong.

This pattern sparked countless fights between my partner and me over the years. But I never stopped to question why these situations bothered me so deeply. I blamed my partner, believing it was his responsibility to stand up for me.

One particular example stands out. A friend in his circle liked paying for every group dinner with his credit card to rack up rewards points. On paper, harmless. In my body, it lit me up. If you know me, you'd know I'm a coupon and reward collector, too.

So one day, I asked my partner why he didn't defend me when I offered to pay for dinner so everyone could reimburse me instead. His response? "I'll just give you a few dollars so you don't have to worry about the credit card rewards."

But it wasn't about the rewards.

It was about fairness.

About not letting one person monopolize the benefits while others get nothing.

About inclusion. About feeling too small to speak up.

If you've ever told yourself *it's not a big deal* while everything inside you screams that it is—you already know what I was living with.

WHEN EVERYTHING FINALLY MADE SENSE

In 2023, I started experiencing neck pain, numbness, and tingling in my fingers. At first, I thought it was the computer overuse from my day job. You might know that inner monologue:

I'm fine. It's just stress. I just need to manage better.

But the symptoms didn't pass; they escalated. My grip weakened until I could barely hold a coffee mug without spilling. I tried everything—physical therapy, posture correction, ergonomic setups, heat, ice, and rest. Each time, I gave myself the same pep talk:

If I just push through a little more, if I just optimize—I'll be okay.

I wasn't okay. The pain sharpened. The numbness spread. Everyday tasks became impossible.

Months later, in 2024, I underwent neck surgery—damaged discs out, titanium implants in.

Recovery was painfully slow. I could barely move. I couldn't bathe myself. Because the surgeon went in through the front of my neck, my throat was swollen and tender. Speaking hurt, and swallowing was work. Turning my head took planning. My body was still, and my mind had nowhere left to hide.

That's when the dark thoughts came.

Was this connected to the assault I survived years ago? Did someone hurt my neck then? Am I paying the price now for someone else's violence?

I wasn't making a medical claim; I was revealing where my brain went when it was desperate for a reason. When you've been hurt, your mind will work overtime trying to make your pain make sense —even if that story quietly blames you.

I was furious. But I didn't understand how deep that fury went until a summer BBQ we were invited to. I could not attend because of my condition.

My partner asked me what he should say when people inquired about my surgery. Then, so casually, he said, "Should I just say it was from bad posture?"

BAD POSTURE! Are you freaking serious?

At that moment, it felt like he was treating my pain as an embarrassment he needed to repackage for public consumption. Not a real wound. Not a loss. Just… bad posture.

I snapped. I was infuriated, ready to tear him apart with my words. And I did.

If you've ever exploded and then thought, *Where the hell did THAT come from?* Then you already know what happened next.

Hours later, instead of justifying my reaction, I finally investigated it. The surgery had stripped me of my dignity, my independence, and my entire year. And underneath all of that was a belief I hadn't wanted to look at:

My pain only counts if it's easy for other people to understand.

I don't matter unless my story is convenient.

That's when I finally noticed a pattern. Suddenly, other memories lined up like dominoes.

Years earlier, when the detective called about my case (Chapter 2) and said, "We have more important cases to handle," it sent the same message:

You don't matter. You're not worth our time.

So, of course, I got furious when my partner's friend hoarded credit card points. Of course, I was enraged when my partner suggested calling my surgery "bad posture."

It was never just about the points. Or the comment. All of these moments echoed the same core injustice:

- People minimizing my pain
- People smoothing over my story so they didn't have to feel uncomfortable
- And me learning to go along with it

That's how deep this shit goes. The hidden monsters don't show up wearing name tags. They lurk in offhand comments, group dynamics, and "jokes," and *it's not a big deal.* They live in the little ways you're trained to package yourself as "easy-going," "low-maintenance," and "not a problem."

I learned something I can't unlearn: your hidden wounds don't stay hidden. They leak into everything—your health, your relationships, your decisions. They show up in the most unexpected moments and smack you in the face.

If you don't tend to them, they infest your whole life—just like mold behind a wall.

That's why I do this work now. I know the cost of staying silent. I don't want you paying that cost for another year of your life.

THE SCIENCE BEHIND OUR THOUGHT PATTERNS

Here's what's happening under the hood.

Your brain changes with what you repeat. Every thought is a step. Walk it often enough, and it turns into a path. Worry and self-criticism dig ruts. Focus, gratitude, and self-compassion lay fresh tracks.

Most of this wiring happens below the surface, which is why habits feel automatic. But **repetition** is how you take the wheel.

Think of your mind as a vast city built on ancient ruins. The streets and buildings you see today—your current thoughts and reactions—are built on layer after layer of older foundations. When something triggers you, it's rarely just about that moment. It's like pulling a thread on a sweater; what looks small is tied into a whole network of experiences, beliefs, and patterns over time.

The good news? Cities can be redesigned. So can neural pathways.

Start tiny. Even a few minutes a day of practicing a different thought, a different response, begins to carve a new route. Every repetition is a vote for who you're becoming.

OUR CHILDHOOD OPERATING SYSTEM

These pathways start early. By grade school, many of our "default settings" are already formed by family, culture, and everyday moments. One look at a family gathering, and suddenly, you're 13 again. That's not weakness; that's your nervous system pulling up the fastest familiar route it learned to keep you safe.

Think of your inner "map" as the brain and body's guide for safety, built from thousands of small lessons: the rules at home, the tone at school, and what your culture calls "strong" or "too much."

Practice turns those lessons into automatic routes.

Overwork to feel worthy. Shrink to keep peace. Smile to hide hurt.

Powerful, yes. Permanent, no.

Some routes run so deep they echo across generations. We inherit patterns in two ways:

(i) **we learn them** (from what got rewarded, what got punished, what stayed unspoken)

(ii) **we carry them** (in a stress system shaped by what our families lived through)

As a kid, you don't ask, *Is this healthy?* You ask, *How do I stay safe and stay connected?* So you become what the environment requires —quiet, useful, easy, invisible, and on guard. Later, your nervous system keeps running that code even when your life has changed. That's not a flaw. It's outdated programming.

Your history isn't destiny. It's information. **Receipts.** Proof of what you (and your family) already paid to survive, not what you still owe.

So we look back, not to get stuck, but to see what got installed so we can update it.

Alarms can be recalibrated. Maps can be redrawn.

Start with the smallest move. When the old route lights up, name it: *Oh, this is my "I'm too much" route.* Take one slow breath. Soften your shoulders. Then choose one tiny new action:

One honest sentence, one boundary, one request for help, one kinder thought toward yourself.

Practice for weeks, and the old urge loosens its grip. Practice for months, and the new response starts showing up on its own. The right people in your corner make the practice easier.

You're not broken; you're patterned. And patterns can change.

For a lot of men, that "map" came with an extra set of rules about pain—and about what you're allowed to feel.

WHY THIS HITS MEN SO HARD (AND WHY WOMEN FEEL IT TOO)

If you're a man reading this, there's a good chance your childhood software came with a few quiet laws:

Don't cry.

Don't talk about it.

Don't make it a big deal.

Be strong. Fix it. Move on.

Maybe no one said those exact words, but you remember the look. The teasing. The silence. The way the room changed when someone got emotional. The way boys who showed feelings were called "dramatic," "needy," "weak," and "too sensitive."

So you learned to translate.

- Pain became, "I'm fine."
- Fear became, "I'm just tired."
- Loneliness became, "I've just been busy."

Under all of that, a message often gets installed:

Your pain is only acceptable if it's invisible, fixable, or funny.

If it's big and complicated, keep it to yourself.

When my partner suggested telling people my neck surgery was "from bad posture," I was furious—and I had every right to be. It felt like he was shrinking my pain down to something neat and harmless.

If I zoom out, I see his training and his wiring:

Keep it simple. Keep it light. Don't talk about trauma at a BBQ. Don't make people uncomfortable. Repackage it.

That doesn't excuse the minimization. It does explain the software that a lot of men are running on.

If you're a man, you might recognize yourself here:

- You downplay your own symptoms until they're screaming.
- You joke about stress instead of saying, "I'm not okay."
- You change the subject when someone else's pain feels too real.
- You love people deeply, but you keep your inner world on lockdown.

From the outside, it all looks "fine." Inside, it often feels exhausting, numb, or quietly angry that no one seems to notice how much you're holding.

You're not broken. You're patterned. You were trained to survive by shrinking your inner life.

The problem is, stigma doesn't just keep things "private." It keeps them **untreated**. It turns wounds into mold—growing in the dark, spreading into your sleep, your work, your relationships, and your body.

Investigating your thought patterns isn't about becoming someone who spills everything to everyone. It's about finally telling yourself the truth:

This hurts.

This matters.

I deserve help.

I don't have to carry this alone.

That one shift—from *I should handle it,* to *I'm allowed to name it*—is often where everything finally starts to make sense.

BECOMING A THOUGHT DETECTIVE

This is why we need to act like detectives of our own thoughts. In previous chapters, we talked about tracking thoughts and interrupting negative spirals. But if we don't step back and analyze the patterns, how will we know what needs upgrading?

Here's an example of how we can analyze our thought patterns:

1. **Curiosity over judgment**: Treat your thoughts like clues, not verdicts. Be the detective, not the critic.

Say, *Oh, here's the "I'm behind" thought again,* instead of *Ugh, why am I like this?*

2. **Pattern recognition**: Track when, where, and with whom certain thoughts show up. Look for repeats.

This pops up after scrolling social media at night, or *I think this when I'm around my older sibling.*

3. **Root cause identification**: Keep asking "why" beneath the reaction or body sensation you're experiencing until you find the **core belief or fear your brain is protecting.**

Why does this thought hit so hard? → Because I'm afraid I'll be left out.

But why does being left out hurt so much? → Because when I was eight, nobody picked me for the game, and I stood alone by the fence.

Because my brain learned, "I'm left out: I don't matter."

This helps us understand why a "small" moment feels like an earthquake.

Investigation isn't about beating yourself up. It's about finally seeing the full picture so you can choose differently.

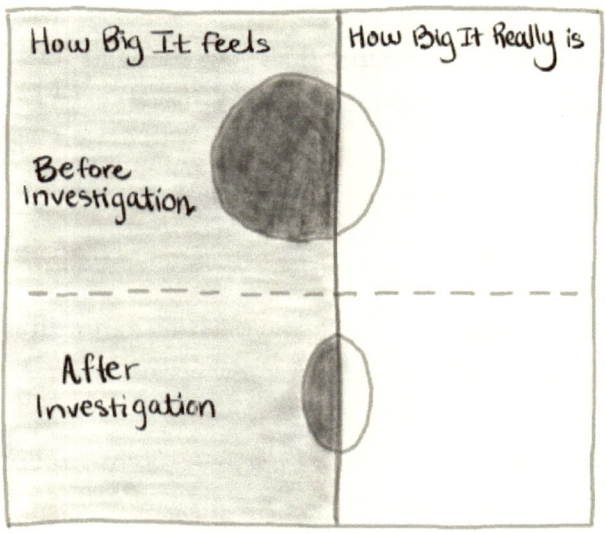

LEARNING FROM HISTORY'S GREAT INVESTIGATORS

"Nothing in life is to be feared; it is only to be understood."

Marie Curie didn't just say that. She lived it. When doors closed to her because she was a woman, she didn't stop. She found a clandestine "Flying University" and kept learning. She studied invisible forces with steady curiosity and changed the world.

We can do the same with our thoughts. Instead of fearing them, we can investigate them. Thought patterns are like invisible currents in that you can't see them, but you can trace where they pull you. Curie's lesson is simple and brave—don't run from the unknown; study it.

Carl Jung did exactly that with his inner world. After his break with Freud, he spent years recording dreams, images, and reflections—work that became the *Red Book*. It wasn't tidy. It was honest, detailed, and relentless. He treated his mind like a landscape to be mapped, not a monster to be avoided.

James Baldwin shows us the social zoom-out. In *Notes of a Native Son*, he examined his anger—where it started in his life and how it connected to racism and the world around him. His courage was in naming the pattern and placing it in context. Our thoughts don't form in a vacuum; they grow in culture, in family, and in history.

Francis Bacon, often called the father of the scientific method, warned about "idols," which are the mental biases that distort what we see. His message: if you don't question your favorite stories, your mind will keep bending reality to fit them.

You don't need a lab coat to do this. I'm inviting you to become a loving scientist of your own mind. Not cold, not clinical—loving.

Notice what repeats. Get curious about what it protects. Test tiny new moves.

Understanding doesn't excuse harm or erase pain. It gives you choices.

THE KITCHEN COUNTER OF YOUR MIND

Think of your thoughts like a cluttered kitchen counter at the end of a long day.

On top are the obvious things—dirty dishes, a half-finished drink. These are your loud thoughts: *I'm so behind. I'm so tired. I don't want to deal with this.*

But underneath the dishes might be unopened bills, letters you've been avoiding, or a form you keep meaning to fill out. Those are your deeper anxieties and unprocessed emotions: shame, grief, anger, and fear.

Ignoring the clutter doesn't make it disappear. It just means you keep cooking around it.

Same with your mind. Until you look under the pile—*Whose voice is this? What am I afraid of here?*—you're just rearranging the mess.

Halting negative patterns (H) is like pushing the dishes aside so nothing spills. Investigating (I) is opening the mail. Until we look into *why* spirals happen, we're just walking around like zombies.

When we consciously investigate thought patterns, we activate our brain's pattern recognition network. This isn't just one brain structure—not just the hippocampus or the amygdala—but a collection of brain structures working together to help you recognize patterns.

128

These networks are like your brain's CSI team—they collect evidence, analyze patterns, and solve the mystery of why certain thoughts keep recurring. You can literally see the difference in brain scans when someone moves from autopilot to curious observation.

In simpler terms, when we take time to understand why we think the way we do, we activate the part of our brain responsible for making conscious choices rather than automatic reactions.

YOUR INVESTIGATION PROTOCOL

Let's summarize how we can analyze our thoughts better.

1. **Name the pattern**. What thoughts keep coming back?
2. **Track the triggers**. When did it start? Where? What situations activate it?
3. **Identify the voices**. Whose voice are you listening to? Parents? Partners? Teachers who told you that you'd never measure up?
4. **Map the connections**. Where else do these thoughts show up in your life?
5. **Trace the roots**. What earlier experiences share this emotional signature?
6. **Connect the dots**. How is this negative thought pattern trying to protect you?

Remember, you don't have to solve everything in one sitting. The act of questioning already activates your conscious brain.

Over time, when that old thought pops up again, your brain will start to connect the dots faster. You'll recognize it sooner. The pattern will feel less like "the truth" and more like "an old file I've seen before."

Only through understanding can we create lasting change. So take a moment to go through this investigation protocol with just one recurring thought.

Recap:

- Your mind builds pathways based on what you repeat. Thoughts become trails; trails become highways.
- By early school age, you're already running on "childhood software" shaped by family, culture, and survival strategies.
- Men, especially, are often trained to minimize and hide their pain, which keeps wounds untreated and festering.
- Investigating your thoughts lets you see patterns instead of being ruled by them.
- Conscious investigation of thought patterns creates new neural connections that help us respond rather than react.

BRAIN NOTES: BRAIN DETECTIVE NETWORK

Pattern Recognition Networks in Action

When you investigate your thought patterns, you activate what neuroscientists call pattern recognition networks. Unlike single brain structures (like the amygdala or hippocampus), these networks involve multiple brain regions working together, like a CSI team for your mind. Research using electrocorticography shows these networks light up when we consciously examine why we think the way we do.

> **Try This:** After noticing a negative thought, place your hand on your forehead and ask yourself, *Where have I encountered this thought before?* This simple action pairs physical touch with mental investigation, creating a tiny habit anchor that activates your brain's pattern recognition system.

Your Brain's CEO

The prefrontal cortex becomes more active when you investigate your thoughts. This region helps you make conscious choices rather than react on autopilot. Harvard Neuroscience Lab research shows that thought patterns create actual neuronal pathways like well-worn trails in a forest—the more you think a certain way, the deeper these trails become.

> **Try This:** Each morning after brushing your teeth (anchor),

identify just one recurring thought (tiny behavior) and ask yourself, *Whose voice is it, really?* (investigation). Then, give yourself a small nod of acknowledgement (celebration). This tiny habit activates your prefrontal cortex, strengthening your ability to recognize thought patterns throughout the day.

Childhood Operating Systems

By early school age, we've already developed core belief systems that influence how we interpret the world. These early patterns become default settings in our mental operating systems—we run our adult lives on childhood software.

> **Try This:** When triggered by a situation, take one deep breath (anchor) and ask yourself, *How old do I feel right now?* (tiny behavior). This micro-moment of awareness helps identify when you're operating from childhood programming, allowing your adult brain to respond rather than react.

Generational Thought Patterns

Dr. Rachel Yehuda's groundbreaking research shows how trauma responses can be passed down through generations, affecting how we react to situations in the present. These inherited patterns can influence our thoughts without our awareness.

> **Try This:** Create a "thought investigation station" by designating a specific chair or spot in your home. Whenever you sit in that designated spot (anchor), spend just 30 seconds

examining a single recurring thought (tiny behavior). This environmental trigger makes investigation automatic rather than requiring willpower.

The Investigation Protocol

Just as archaeologists carefully excavate ancient cities to understand civilizations, we need to investigate our thought patterns to understand our reactions. The brain responds powerfully to systematic approaches.

Try This: After your daily shower (anchor), name one thought pattern (tiny behavior) and ask one "why" question about it (investigation). Then, physically tap your temple twice (celebration). This sequence creates a complete habit loop that strengthens with repetition, making thought investigation an automatic part of your day.

Remember, investigation isn't about fixing—it's about understanding. By approaching your thoughts with scientific curiosity rather than fear, you activate the brain networks that allow for lasting change, one tiny investigation at a time.

CHAPTER 8
LETTER "N" – NURTURE NEW PERSPECTIVES

WHEN YOUR CAREFULLY BUILT LIFE CRUMBLES

Moving to a new country wasn't a fun experiment. My parents uprooted our lives so their kids could have a better education and a better shot.

Back home, I had been the good student. Top of the class. Teachers knew my name for the right reasons. My identity felt simple: *smart, hardworking, going somewhere.* I wanted to make their sacrifice worth it.

Then I landed in an American high school where my English was barely functional.

Classrooms blurred into one long hallway of fluorescent lights and fast conversations. Kids laughed at jokes I couldn't catch. Teachers gave instructions, and I heard noise. The textbooks felt heavier than my entire vocabulary.

I went from "top student" to "the girl who doesn't get it" almost overnight.

That wasn't just a change in circumstances. It was a direct hit to my **identity**. And when identity gets shaken, your brain scrambles to make sense of the new data:

Maybe I'm not that smart after all.

Maybe I don't belong here.

Maybe this is where my story ends.

Quietly and efficiently, my brain started rewiring around **failure**.

THE DAY I OVERHEARD I'D BE "JUST ANOTHER DROPOUT"

One afternoon, it all got too loud. I ended up in the nurse's office, lying down, just trying to breathe and make the headache stop. The room was dim. The paper under me crinkled each time I shifted. Outside, lockers slammed, and footsteps echoed between classes.

I wasn't supposed to hear what came next.

Two nurses stood just outside the curtain, talking as if I wasn't there. One of them said, casually, almost like a weather report:

"She will just be another high school dropout."

Not "this is hard for her."

Not "how can we support her?"

Just a prediction. A verdict. A label.

I remember staring at the ceiling tiles, frozen. My throat tightened. Part of me wanted to disappear. Another part wanted to leap up and scream, "You don't know me!"

I just lay there, letting the words etch themselves into my nervous system.

My brain did what brains do: it took that sentence and started building a **story** around it.

Maybe they're right.

*Maybe I **am** going to fail.*

Maybe I'm already too far behind.

That's how fast one careless sentence can become a **neural pathway**.

5 A.M. EXPERIMENTS: TURNING AN INSULT INTO A TRAINING PLAN

That night, I couldn't get the nurse's voice out of my head. *Another High School Dropout.*

I could feel two paths forming inside me: believe her and quietly collapse into that story, or use her words as fuel.

The next morning, my alarm went off at 5:00 a.m.

Everyone else was asleep. The house was dark and quiet. I shuffled to the kitchen table with a stack of newspapers and a dictionary that seemed bigger than my head.

There was nothing glamorous about it.

No montage music. Just ink-smudged fingers and heavy eyelids. I circled words I didn't know, looked them up one by one, wrote the definitions down, and tried to pronounce them in my thick accent. Sometimes I had to look up the same word three times before it stuck.

During the day, I camped out in the library. After school, a math teacher stayed back and walked me through problems that looked like a foreign language—because in many ways, they were.

At night, I turned on the TV—not to relax, but to **train**. And here's the part that still makes me smile: I watched *Barney*.

Yes, the big purple dinosaur. A show meant for preschoolers. Kids born in this country had outgrown it years ago. But the simple language, the repetition, the songs—I could follow that. I watched Barney not as a child, but as a teenager trying to rebuild her world one sentence at a time.

None of this looked heroic from the outside. It just looked like a girl hunched over a dictionary, a library table, and a children's show.

But from the brain's point of view, this was **high-intensity training**: repetition, struggle, tiny wins. Over and over.

Day by day, the "dropout" comment stopped feeling like a prophecy and started feeling like a **data point**—one person's untrained guess in a moment when I was at my lowest.

It was no longer, *This is who you are.*

It became: *This is where you are right now. What are you going to do with it?*

Years later, I graduated in the **top five** of my class. Not because I was magically gifted.

Because I **trained** toward a different outcome, while my brain was screaming, *You're behind,* or, *This is too hard,* or, *People like you don't catch up!*

The nurse's sentence didn't disappear. I just refused to let it be the final line of my story.

FROM MUTING TO NURTURING (AND HOW IT HELPED ME LATER)

In Chapter 6, we talked about **halting** spirals—what I think of as muting the inner critic.

Muting is what you do when the old story is screaming in your ear. You catch that harsh, familiar voice, you name it for what it is—old wiring, not absolute truth—and you turn the emotional volume down just enough so you can breathe again. It's powerful, but it's **temporary**. Muting is like taking your hands off your own throat so you can actually get air. You're not healed yet, but you're no longer being strangled by the old story.

What I did at 5 a.m. in high school was the next layer—what I now call **nurturing**.

Nurturing means you don't just turn down the old voice; you **feed a new one**. You give your brain new experiences, new proof, and new patterns to wire around. Every newspaper article I stumbled through, every math problem my teacher walked me through, every *Barney* episode I repeated until the phrases stuck—that was nurturing. I wasn't arguing with "you'll be a dropout." I was **answering it with training**.

The nurse's sentence shifted from a verdict to a data point. A data point can tell you, "This is how someone is seeing you right now," or "This is where your skills are at this moment." It can sting, but it's still just **information**.

It is information you can work with. Years later, when a mentor looked me in the eye and said, "You're not ready," that old wound lit up. My brain instantly recognized the pattern: *Here we go again. Someone is writing my ending for me.*

My stomach dropped. My chest tightened. For a moment, it felt like being back in that nurse's office, listening to my future being decided without me.

But then another part of me woke up—the part that remembered what I'd already survived.

I knew I had to regroup and find my inner compass again. I had to reconnect with myself:

- *Where is the Khai I know?*
- *The girl who didn't speak English but somehow worked her way to be in the top five.*
- *The woman who survived an assault with no justice and kept going.*
- *The MFing **beast** who says, "Just watch me."*

That mentor was hitting a raw nerve, but this time something was different: I had **receipts** of what I'd overcome.

The truth is, I didn't get that job. There's no fairy-tale twist. The door closed. It hurt. I questioned my abilities, my path, and my worth.

But thanks to those 5 a.m. mornings, I'd learned something important back in high school. Painful feedback doesn't get to be the final word. It gets to be the **starting point** of a training plan.

So I went back to what I knew: when I feel lost, I **serve**.

At the time, I was teaching basic tech skills to women who had been previously incarcerated. We sat in a small room with donated laptops, practicing emails, resumes, and job searches. Some of them had never had anyone look them in the eye and say, "You can learn this."

For a few hours at a time, my mentor's words faded into the background. These women, their courage, their fear, and their second chances became the main story.

As I helped them create their first email accounts, watched them send resumes, and saw their pride when something finally clicked, I remembered:

*I know how to **break down complex things** so people can understand them.*

I know how to believe in people others have written off—because I've been that person.

I enjoy helping people level up.

That, too, is nurturing.

I wasn't just building skills for them; I was rebuilding my own sense of purpose. The more I showed up for those women, the less power that "you're not ready" sentence had over me. It was still a data point. But it wasn't my identity.

By the time the opportunity at AWS (Amazon Web Services) came around, I was showing up from a different place. Not as someone begging to be picked, but as someone who knew, *I bring something real to the table. I do hard things. I help people grow.*

Remembering that I was a survivor didn't magically hand me that job. It changed how I met the setback and how I prepared afterward. Less spinning in shame. More grounded, quiet confidence built on history: *I have done impossible things before. I know how to train my way through this.*

If you look closely, this is THINK already at work. First, I **Tracked** the stories in my head—the nurse's voice, the mentor's voice. Then I **Halted** the spiral long enough to say, *Wait. This is not the whole truth.* I **Investigated** what was actually being revealed: real gaps, yes, but also real strengths. And I chose to **Nurture** a different narrative through concrete action—5 a.m. study, serving in the shelter, and showing up again.

Soon, we'll dive into **K: Keep Practicing**. For now, it's enough to see this: your brain can learn a new way to respond, even when it feels like history is repeating itself.

STEPPING OUTSIDE MY BUBBLE

The more I struggled with English when I was in high school, the more I started to see other people differently.

The quiet student in the back who never raised his hand? Maybe English wasn't his first language either. The kid who skipped class a lot? Maybe she was dealing with chaos at home that would break most adults. The "lazy" student might be exhausted from working nights.

My old identity—"the smart one"—had kept me in a bubble. I assumed I understood everyone's story from the outside.

This experience smashed that illusion.

For the first time, I **felt** what it was like to be misunderstood, underestimated, and written off with one phrase: "just another dropout."

That pain became a doorway. It made me more curious, more compassionate, and more willing to pause before labeling someone else. Without realizing it, I was training two things at once: my **cognitive skills** (language, math, study habits) and my **perspective** —how I saw myself and the people around me.

This is the heart of mental well-being and leadership: not just what you *can* do, but how you *see*.

THE NEUROSCIENCE OF A GROWTH MINDSET

Psychologist **Carol Dweck** introduced the ideas of **fixed mindset** and **growth mindset**.

- A **fixed mindset** says, *My abilities are what they are. If I fail, it proves I'm not good enough.*
- A **growth mindset** says, *My abilities can be developed. If I fail, it shows me where I need to train.*

In her research with students, she found something simple but powerful. When kids were praised for being "smart," they became more afraid of hard problems. Struggle felt like proof that maybe they weren't smart after all. When kids were praised for their effort and strategies ("You worked really hard on that," "You tried a new way"), they were more willing to tackle difficult tasks. Struggle meant they were **learning**, not failing.

Brain imaging studies later echoed this pattern. People who leaned more toward a growth mindset showed **stronger brain responses after mistakes**, especially in regions involved in learning and error correction. Their brains were staying in "learning mode." People with more of a fixed mindset often showed weaker responses to errors, as if their brain had already decided, *There's no point; this just proves I'm bad at this.*

Here's why this matters when you're in pain.

When you believe *I can get better with effort,* your brain treats difficulty as a **signal to engage**, not just a threat. Your amygdala—the alarm system—still reacts to stress, but your prefrontal cortex—the part involved in planning and decision-making—stays more online. You're more able to pause, think, and choose your next move instead of shutting down.

A growth mindset doesn't mean you enjoy failing. It means your brain doesn't stop at *this hurts.* It moves toward *what can I learn here?*

Back in that 5 a.m. kitchen, and later when my mentor said, "You're not ready," I didn't know the term "growth mindset." But I was living it. Every time I chose to treat a painful comment as information and build a small training plan around it—studying, serving, trying again—I was sending a clear signal to my brain:

Struggle means we're in training, not that we're broken.

That is a different kind of wiring. You are not your circumstances. I need you to say it out loud.

Choose to respond differently.

"Everything can be taken from a man but one thing: the last of the human freedoms—to choose one's attitude in any given set of circumstances, to choose one's own way." – Viktor Frankl

HELEN KELLER'S POWERFUL LESSON

Helen Keller was both blind and deaf before she turned two. For years, the world around her was there but locked away—no shared language, no way to easily say, "I'm here. I matter." Her teacher, Anne Sullivan, didn't change Helen's circumstances. She changed Helen's access to them.

When Anne finally broke through with the concept of "water"—spelling it into Helen's hand while pumping water over it—something woke up. That connection didn't erase pain or limitation, but it gave Helen a way to *work with* reality instead of being crushed by it.

She didn't choose her disability. She chose what to do with her life inside it.

That's perspective.

Like Helen Keller, we all face moments when our world seems dark and limiting. You may feel trapped in your own prison of negative thoughts. But just as she learned to see the world through touch and vibration, we can learn to view our challenges not as walls but as doorways to new understanding and strength. The world cannot see how great you are if you give up, if you stay stuck, or if you cling to a fixed story about who you are.

You don't have to love what happened or call it a gift. But you can treat it as **training data**—evidence that you are already the kind of person who can do hard things, learn new patterns, and, over time, turn pain into fuel.

In the words of Helen Keller, "The only thing worse than being blind is having sight but no vision."

REMEMBERING YOU'RE A SURVIVOR (YOUR TURN)

If you've been reading up to this point, you've walked through some heavy places—rejection, shame, burnout, betrayal. You might still be in one of those valleys right now.

So let this chapter be a turn.

I'm not asking you to copy my story or Helen Keller's. You don't need a nurse's office moment, or a perfect exam score, or a mentor who tells you you're not ready, or an AWS badge, or a world-famous teacher to qualify as a survivor.

You already have your own 5 a.m. moments.

Think back to a time when you were sure you wouldn't make it through—and yet, somehow, you did. Maybe no one else even noticed. Maybe there were no trophies or LinkedIn posts. But you kept going when quitting would have been easier.

That counts.

From a brain perspective, those memories are not just sentimental. They are **evidence**—neural proof that you have done hard things before. When you deliberately bring those memories back online, you're reminding your nervous system: *We have been here. We did not die. We adapted. We grew.*

You are reactivating a network of **resilience**, not just replaying the pain.

You can even run a quiet, mini version of THINK in your head:

- **Track** what this moment is saying to you. What's the sentence looping right now?
- **Halt** long enough to notice *this is a story, not a law of physics.*
- **Investigate** what's actually true: Where am I today? What is this showing me about what I need? What did my past survival moments prove about me?
- **Nurture** your next step with one small act—send the email, ask for help, study for 20 minutes, or show up for someone else the way you wish someone had shown up for you.

You don't have to fix everything at once. You just have to **catch the story, pause, get curious, and choose one small way to train differently**.

The next time a "you're not ready" moment hits—whether it's a failed interview, a breakup, a layoff, or a health scare—pause.

Mute the panic long enough to remember:

I've survived before. I've adapted before. I've already been the person who trains their way through "impossible."

You might not fully believe it in that moment. That's okay. You don't have to *feel* strong to practice acting like a survivor.

The science says your brain will follow the patterns you repeat. Your story says you've already done this, more than once.

If you take nothing else from this chapter, take this line you can borrow the next time it feels like too much: **I am a survivor. I will get through this.**

Recap:

- Nurturing new perspectives is not "positive thinking." It is practicing a new response when the old story shows up.
- You can turn an insult, rejection, or setback into a training plan instead of a verdict about who you are.

- Moving from muting to nurturing means you stop abandoning yourself to keep the peace and start honoring your needs, boundaries, and voice.
- Like technology, your brain needs regular updates. New inputs create new perspectives, and new perspectives build pathways that weaken outdated patterns over time.
- A growth mindset is a practice: feedback becomes information for adjustment, not proof of unworthiness.
- Remembering you are a survivor is a perspective shift that restores agency and forward motion.

BRAIN NOTES: THE NEUROSCIENCE OF PERSPECTIVE SHIFTS

A Shift in Mindset

Your brain physically changes when you adopt new perspectives. When you shift from a fixed to a growth mindset, neural networks associated with learning become more robust while activity in your amygdala decreases. This isn't just psychological; it's a measurable biological transformation.

> **Try This**: When facing a challenge, say to yourself, *I'm not good at this **yet**,* instead of *I'm not good at this.* The simple word "yet" activates different neural pathways, triggering your brain to release more BDNF (brain-derived neurotrophic factor), which supports new neural connections.

Your Attention Shapes Your Reality

Your reticular activating system, or RAS, filters millions of sensory inputs, allowing only a tiny fraction into your conscious awareness. Your repeated focus literally programs this filter, leading you to notice evidence that confirms your existing beliefs while overlooking contradictory information.

> **Try This**: Set a tiny daily alarm labeled *"What's going right?"* When it sounds, identify one positive aspect of your current

situation. This micro-habit gradually reprograms your RAS to detect opportunities rather than just threats.

The Neurochemistry of Possibility

When you believe something is possible, your brain releases dopamine—not just a pleasure chemical but a motivation molecule that energizes action. Simultaneously, cortisol levels decrease, allowing your prefrontal cortex to think more creatively and see solutions instead of just problems.

> **Try This**: Before bed, write down one small win from your day. This 30-second habit triggers the release of dopamine, which strengthens neural pathways associated with achievement, making your brain more likely to spot opportunities tomorrow.

Social Connection Rewires Neural Circuits

Helping others activates your brain's reward pathways while reducing activity in stress-processing regions. When you volunteer or support others (like teaching technology to formerly incarcerated women), your brain produces oxytocin, which not only feels good but actually enhances neuroplasticity, or your brain's ability to form new connections.

> **Try This**: Create a "contribution trigger"—a tiny action that reminds you to help someone else. Place a paper clip in your pocket each morning; when you touch it during the day, find one small way to assist another person. This builds

neural pathways that associate helping others with personal reward.

Perspective Switching as Neural Exercise

Deliberately adopting different viewpoints strengthens connections between your prefrontal cortex and limbic system, improving emotional regulation. Like cross-training for your brain, this practice builds cognitive flexibility, or your ability to adapt to changing circumstances.

Try This: When stuck in negative thinking, spend 30 seconds imagining how someone you admire would view your situation. This brief mental shift activates different neural networks, creating alternative pathways that bypass entrenched negative thinking patterns.

CHAPTER 9
LETTER "K" – KEEP PRACTICING

YOUR BRAIN'S INCREDIBLE RENOVATION PROJECT

You swear you won't snap tonight. Then your kid spills milk, or your teammate sends a snarky message at 9:47 p.m., and boom—there's that sharp voice again. Or maybe you promise to be kinder to yourself, but that old loop—*I'm not enough*—slides right back in.

I've been there. I've found myself lashing out at my partner in moments of frustration, despite my promises to create space between triggers and responses. The gap between who we want to be and who we actually are in heated moments can be maddening.

While you're beating yourself up about these "failures," your brain is in the middle of an incredible renovation project. And every time you simply notice that gap—even when you mess up—you are kickstarting powerful changes at the cellular level.

153

When clients tell me, "I reverted back," I smile and congratulate them on noticing. Awareness is a big win. Most people revert without seeing it. The moment you can see the loop, you can change it.

We're not trying to become brand-new people. We're updating our inner operating system—rewiring patterns installed years ago.

If you're a dad who takes a breath instead of losing it after stepping on a LEGO at 2 a.m., a manager who stays grounded when someone takes a cheap shot in a meeting, a nurse who pauses before answering a buzzing alarm in hour eleven, or a mom who catches one unhelpful thought at the sink—you're practicing.

You're wiring the next version of yourself, one microscopic choice at a time.

THE DANCE PARTY IN YOUR HEAD

Awkward.
New. Fragile.

Again. Again.
and again.

Let's go behind the scenes.

Your brain isn't a static lump. It's a living construction site with billions of tiny workers, called neurons, constantly reshaping.

More join the
Rhythm.

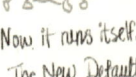

Now it runs itself.
The New Default

When you try something new—like pausing before you fire back at a snarky text—neurons start forming fresh connections, like dancers reaching for each other's hands. At first, it's fingertips: awkward, slow, easy to break.

But repetition recruits more dancers. The rhythm smooths out. And eventually, the choreography runs without you thinking about it.

Neuroscientists call this "long-term potentiation," or LTP: **when neurons fire together repeatedly, their connection strengthens.**

It's your brain saying, *This matters—make it easier next time.*

Every rep counts, even the clumsy ones.

YOUR BRAIN'S SUPERHIGHWAY SYSTEM

Practice doesn't just connect dancers. It upgrades the road between them. Your brain wraps frequently used pathways in a fatty substance called **myelin**. Think of myelin as insulation on a wire or asphalt on a dirt road.

More myelin = faster signals, less energy wasted.

The exact speed varies by pathway, but the message is simple: **repetition lays down insulation, and insulation builds speed and reliability.** That's why new habits feel clumsy at first and smoother later. Under the surface, your brain is paving a superhighway.

This is why early practice feels awkward. You can't see the foundation yet, but it's being poured. Most people give up too soon during this phase because they don't understand the brain's construction schedule. It's like learning a new language: at first it takes enormous effort and feels like nothing's happening—yet the struggle is laying an invisible foundation.

CLEARING SPACE SO THE STRONG CAN GROW

Your brain isn't just building new roads. It's also clearing old ones that no longer serve you. This process is called "long-term depression," or LTD (not to be confused with the mood disorder). It's your brain's way of turning down unused circuits so healthier ones can grow. Less noise. Better signal. It isn't punishment; it's efficient housekeeping.

So when an old reaction still shows up, especially under stress, it doesn't mean you're back at zero. It means the old road still has traffic. The invisible win is noticing sooner, interrupting faster, and choosing the new route again. Over time, what you don't practice fades—and what you repeat becomes your default.

TINY WINS, BIG WIRING

Remember when you first learned to cook? Burnt garlic. Mushy pasta. Then, after enough reps—yes, including watching a few Gordon Ramsay YouTube tutorials—your hands started to know what to do. That's what tiny wins do: small repetitions that turn effort into instinct.

Bruce Lee said it best: *"I fear not the man who has practiced ten thousand kicks once, but I fear the man who has practiced one kick ten thousand times."* That's **neuroplasticity**—your brain's ability to rewire through repeated experience. You're not stuck with the brain you were born with. This isn't feel-good talk; it's neuroscience. And it's why **small, consistent practice** beats occasional intensity.

LEARNING FROM THE MASTERS OF PRACTICE

Katherine Johnson, the brilliant NASA mathematician whose calculations helped send astronauts safely to the moon, checked and rechecked her work thousands of times. Her life was about consistency. Every calculation was a practice in excellence.

Johnson, who faced both racial and gender discrimination in the 1960s, understood something profound about the brain: focused, repetitive practice builds stronger neural pathways in areas associated with precision and attention. Her work wasn't just about math. It was about training her brain to be exceptional through consistent practice despite unfavorable conditions.

When Beethoven began losing his hearing—a devastating blow for any musician—he didn't give up composing. Instead, he sawed the legs off his piano so he could feel the vibrations through the floor as he played. Each day, despite his increasing deafness, he found new ways to practice his craft, creating some of his most profound work after he could no longer hear.

Beethoven's story demonstrates how our brains can form new pathways even when old ones are blocked. Over time, his brain rewired itself to process music through touch rather than sound, showing the incredible adaptability of our neural networks when faced with challenges.

BECOMING THE BOSS OF YOUR THOUGHTS (IT'S A TEAM SPORT)

As you practice the THINK framework, your "coach" brain (prefrontal cortex) gets better at guiding the alarm centers (e.g., amygdala). It's not one part versus another—it's a network. Different regions play different roles, like positions on a team. Your job is to help the switchboard hand the ball to the right player at the right time.

Picture this.

You're in a meeting, and someone takes a cheap shot at your team. The old you fires back and regrets it; the rewired you feels the surge, names it, takes one slow breath, and says, "Let's get clear on the goal." That's your network working.

You miss a personal record at the gym. The old you throws more plates on the bar to prove a point and strains a shoulder; the rewired you strips the bar, focuses on form, logs one clean set, and comes back stronger the next week.

Your parents repeat the same question for the fifth time in one day. The old you snaps. The rewired you notices the tightness, puts a hand on your chest, and answers with softness once more.

That's the OS upgrade, right there in the mess. This is your brain's new highway in action. The pathways you've built through consistent practice are now strong enough to override old patterns.

YOUR 30-SECOND BRAIN WORKOUT

Here's a simple but powerful practice: set a timer for just 30 seconds to be alone with your thoughts.

Track one negative thought that keeps showing up. Whatever it may be, just notice it. Don't try to fix everything at once.

Remember, awareness is the first brick. And when you catch yourself "reverting," count it as a rep. You found the loop while you were in it, and that's how we upgrade the OS—one detection, one micro-choice, repeated.

Create a journal to track your tiny wins. Your brain loves evidence. It's constantly gathering data points and adapting with experience. Every attempt—even when you slip back five minutes later—is helping lay those invisible foundations in your brain, and each journal entry reinforces the new pathways you're building.

FALL DOWN. REWIRE. REPEAT.

You will slip. You will snap. You will say things you wish you hadn't and think thoughts you believed you'd "outgrown."

Don't turn a slip into a life story. Make it a signal.

New Year's resolutions often die by March because they depend on motivation instead of understanding how the brain changes. Real habits form over **weeks to months**, not days. The range is wide because people and situations are different.

Your brain is not on a stopwatch. It's building roads.

Old patterns—some installed in childhood—don't vanish. They get weaker while new ones grow stronger. Your job isn't to erase your past. It's to choose which path you feed, again and again, until it becomes the easier route.

Would it be easier to stay stuck in old patterns for the rest of your life? Maybe, at first.

But you'd never discover what your brain—and your life—are actually capable of.

So embrace those invisible wins each day, even when you don't feel like it. Each practice session strengthens your brain for the change you want to see.

Our brains are plastic—they can change and adapt. We're not prisoners of our past experiences. Whatever situations you've had to endure, you can bounce back. I'm a living example!

I'm not promising it'll be easy or that you'll wake up tomorrow feeling amazing. Life, unfortunately, doesn't work that way. But you can become more resilient. And that's something to be proud of.

Keep Practicing

Recap:

- Your brain physically changes with every attempt at new behavior, not just successful ones.
- Long-term potentiation strengthens neural connections with repeated use.

- Myelin is a fatty substance that wraps neural pathways, making them up to three thousand times faster and more efficient.
- Long-term depression is your brain's pruning process that removes unused neural pathways.
- Strengthening the prefrontal cortex-amygdala pathway improves emotional regulation and stress resilience.
- Consistency over intensity. Your brain prefers regular small efforts over sporadic intense ones.

BRAIN NOTES: YOUR BRAIN'S RENOVATION PROJECT

Plasticity 101: LTP, LTD, and Timing (How Reps Stick)

When neurons fire together over and over, their connection strengthens in a process called long-term potentiation, or LTP. When a pathway sits idle or fires out of sync, it can weaken, a process called long-term depression, or LTD. The timing between spikes matters (often called spike-timing-dependent plasticity): arrive together, get stronger; miss the beat, get weaker. This is why focus and consistency matter. You're not just doing a rep—you're teaching your neurons when to light up, together.

> **Try This:** Pick one cue you hit every day (door handle before a meeting, barbell grip before a lift, hand on the fridge). Pair it with the same three-second pause and one clear intention. Teach your brain to fire the right neurons together, on schedule.

Myelin: Speed, Efficiency, and Reliability (Why Reps Feel Easier)

Myelin wraps axons like insulation on a wire. It boosts speed, keeps signals clean, and saves energy. Repetition can drive adaptive myelination. That's one reason skills feel smoother and less tiring with practice. You're laying down insulation where it counts.

Try This: Choose one micro-habit to repeat in the same context daily—two slow exhales before you unmute on a call or one beat of stillness before you answer your child. Same cue, same action, same timing. You're drawing the blueprint for myelin.

Pruning: The Cleanup Crew (Making Space for Better Paths)

As new skills form, your brain trims what you don't use. Microglia, the brain's cleanup cells, help tag and remove extra synapses. This reduces noise and gives strong pathways room to grow. Pruning can feel like *I lost my edge* when an old habit fades, but really, you're making space for better patterns.

Try This: When an old loop appears, label it "pruning in progress." Then do your tiny move: one breath, one written line, one reset rep. Name it. Redirect it.

Networks, Not Just Parts (Alarm, Story, and Switchboard)

Emotion and decision-making ride on networks. The salience network is your switchboard—it spots what matters and helps you switch tasks. The executive network helps you plan, focus, and choose. The default network is your story-brain—active when your mind wanders, when you think about yourself and others, and when you connect dots. Training attention and breathing helps the switchboard hand control to the right player at the right time.

Try this: Do a "Body–Story–Move" check during a trigger.

Body: *What do I feel* (hot face, tight jaw, heavy chest)?
Story: What meaning popped up? *(They don't respect me),* or
what memory is here *(last time, this ended badly)?* Move:
What urge is here *(snap, shut down, fix)?* Pick one word for
each, then choose one small action. You just recruited the
whole network.

HRV: Flexibility You Can Feel (But Not a Report Card)

Heart-rate variability is the tiny changes in time between heart-
beats. Higher resting HRV (i.e., more variation in time between
beats) generally points to a system that can shift gears under stress.
Slow breathing (around six breaths per minute) can nudge HRV up
in the moment and may build flexibility over time. It's a useful
signal, not a grade on your worth. Use it like a dashboard light, not
a verdict.

> **Try This:** Before a tough conversation or a heavy lift, take
> two minutes. Inhale for four counts, exhale for six. If that's
> hard, try three to five. Longer exhales help the nervous
> system settle.

Awareness Is the First Rep (Why "I'm Reverting" Is Good News)

Clients often say, "I thought I was past this. I'm reverting." Here's
the reframe: the moment you notice you're reverting is the rep. You
are building the skill of interrupting and choosing, which is exactly
what durable change needs. This is memory and habit, not moral-
ity. You're not failing; you're learning.

Try This: Keep a "slip log." In less than a minute, jot down three quick lines: the trigger (what set it off), the loop (what you did or thought), and the next tiny move (what you'll try next time). Think of it as your coach's tape to learn from —not a blame list.

How Long Does It Take? (The Honest Timeline)

Habits form over weeks and months. Studies show a wide range because people and contexts differ. Old patterns, some learned in childhood, don't vanish; they get weaker while new ones grow stronger. Your job isn't to erase your past. It's to choose which path you feed, again and again, until it becomes the easy path.

Try This: Pick a 30-day streak for one tiny habit—maybe 30 seconds of thought tracking or a single breath before you speak. Mark each day on your calendar to create a visible chain, and aim to never miss twice.

Consistency Over Intensity

Your brain responds better to brief, consistent practice than to occasional intense efforts. Most New Year's resolutions fail by March because they rely on motivation rather than tiny, sustainable actions that work alongside your brain's natural wiring.

Try This: Create a "tiny wins" journal to record each small attempt at changing a thought pattern. Your brain loves evidence, and each entry reinforces the neural pathways you're building. Even a simple checkmark on your phone calendar can provide the visual proof your brain craves.

PART FOUR
THINK IN ACTION

CHAPTER 10
THE FAMILY BLUEPRINT –
HOW PAST HIJACKS PRESENT

YOUR BRAIN'S OLD CODE: CHILDHOOD PROGRAMMING IS STILL RUNNING THE SHOW.

You don't wake up thinking about your childhood. You wake up thinking about your schedule.

And then something tiny happens—and you feel way more than the moment calls for.

A one-line email that lands like rejection.

A "quick chat" that spikes your pulse.

A teammate's win that somehow makes you feel smaller.

You tell yourself you're being ridiculous. You tell yourself to get it together.

But your nervous system doesn't care about your title. It cares about safety.

And it's using a map that was drawn a long time ago.

When I work with clients, they come to me thinking they know what's wrong: "I'm too sensitive at work." "I can't take feedback." "I ruin every good thing."

But when we follow the thread, we find older wounds—quiet, stubborn, and very alive—steering today's choices. Programs that have been running their life from the shadows.

DAVID: "WHY DO I LOSE IT OVER NOTHING?"

David came to me convinced that he had an anger issue. On paper, he was a high achiever—disciplined, ambitious, and constantly moving. Awards. Promotions. The person others pointed to and said, "That guy's got it together."

At home, it's a different story.

If his partner casually mentioned a friend's new house, David would snap. Not "mildly annoyed." Full heat. Sharp tone. Contempt. Then the crash—shame, confusion, self-disgust.

"Why do I lose it over nothing?" he asked.

David wasn't a "talk about your feelings" guy. If an emotional scene came on TV, he'd roll his eyes: "Here comes the sob story." He worked at least 80 hours a week, chased the next rung, and still felt like he was behind.

But it wasn't nothing.

It was *everything*.

David lost his mom when he was 7.

His dad, drowning in grief, turned to alcohol. One day, David came home bruised and bleeding—bullies had shoved him into concrete blocks, splitting the skin on his face and knees.

His dad screamed:

"Why do you look like hell? What's wrong with you?"

No comfort. No curiosity. Just shame.

David never told him about the bullies. His safe person was gone, and the remaining parent felt unsafe.

Then, when his dad remarried soon after, David was moved out of his bedroom to make room for his new stepsister. Every family photo with his mom disappeared. His stepmom made sure he knew he wasn't measuring up: "How come you didn't get an A? B- isn't good enough."

David didn't just lose his mother. He lost his place in the world.

So he built a new place by achieving.

If he could stay exceptional, he couldn't be replaced. If he could stay ahead, he couldn't disappear.

Thirty years later a casual comment about someone else's success wasn't just "news." It rhymed with the past. And his nervous system responded like it always had:

Protect the wound. Don't get left behind. Your place isn't secure.

And his body reacted like it was protecting his life. Because for a kid who lost his place in the world, belonging can feel like survival.

If you've ever looked fine while feeling like you're fighting inside… you get him.

And if you don't relate to his details, you might relate to his strategy: *Work harder. Stay busy. Don't feel. Don't be needy.*

That's not arrogance. That's protection.

YOUR BRAIN'S SECRET RECORDING

Your brain isn't recording your life like a camera. It records **associations**.

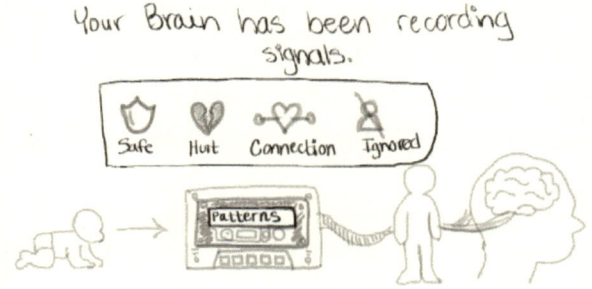

Cue → meaning → response

Tone → danger

Silence → rejection

Authority → shame

Comparison → threat

Emotion makes the recording stick. Repetition makes it automatic.

In psychology, that's conditioning and reinforcement—learning what predicts pain or connection.

In neuroscience, repeated activation strengthens the networks that tend to fire together. Over time, those networks become default pathways.

Some of what we carry is **explicit.** Facts and scenes we can intentionally recall and describe.

Some is **implicit learning.** Conditioned responses, priming effects, habit-like tendencies, and response patterns that shape what we notice and how we react without requiring conscious recall.

We don't always "remember" this kind of learning. We **reenact** it.

That's why our body can mobilize before our mind finishes its sentence.

Under perceived threat, the brain shifts resources: fast detection and protection can dominate, while nuance and reflection get harder to access. This isn't a personality defect. It's how stress physiology works.

A QUICK, GROUNDED NOTE ON EPIGENETICS

If stress is chronic, your body can adapt in ways that make you quicker to detect threats and slower to settle. That can show up in stress hormones (HPA axis), immune/inflammatory signaling, and brain circuits involved in threat and regulation.

Epigenetics is one mechanism that may help explain how experience gets "embedded" without changing your DNA sequence: gene expression can be dialed up or down through regulatory marks such as DNA methylation and histone modifications. The research is complex and often correlational, but the core idea is consistent: long-term conditions can shape long-term settings.

And because these are regulatory systems—not a rewritten DNA code—they can shift over time with sustained changes: recovery, supportive relationships, reduced ongoing stress, and repeated regulation practice.

Your brain isn't trying to sabotage you.

It's trying to protect you with data that's decades old.

YOUR INVISIBLE OPERATING SYSTEM (OS)

Every bias you have, every snap judgment, every person who "just rubs you wrong"—it's connected to a story in your past.

The coworker who reminds you of your critical father.

The manager whose tone hits your "I'm not important" wound.

The person whose confidence makes you shrink because you learned early that taking up space was dangerous.

We think we're objective. We think we're professional.

But in reality, none of us are.

We are all walking around with invisible wounds that color every interaction.

Your brain is an efficient machine. It uses shortcuts (heuristics) to make quick judgments from limited data. It predicts quickly from fragments—tone, posture, facial expressions, and silence. Under stress, it leans harder on what it already knows. It fills in the blanks.

So you stop responding to what's happening now and start responding to what your nervous system predicts is coming next.

That's why two people can sit in the same meeting, hear the same feedback, and have completely different internal experiences.

One hears, "This will help me grow."

The other hears, "I'm about to be rejected."

Same words. Different operating systems.

David's internal operating system (OS) ran on old code:

- If I'm not ahead, I'm not safe.
- If I'm not exceptional, I disappear.
- If someone else wins, I lose.

That code made sense when he was seven. It just didn't get updated.

That's the trap: you can be brilliant, successful, and self-aware... and still be driven by patterns you didn't choose.

Until you see the code.

Once you see it, you can rewrite it.

HOW YOUR OLD CODE SHOWS UP

Most people don't realize they're running a default setting until it starts costing them—energy, relationships, trust.

These aren't personality traits. They're protection strategies your nervous system learned early and then carried forward.

[1] Space Scarcity (Always Giving)

You say yes before you even check in with yourself.

You take the extra meeting. You cover the gap. You pick up the slack.

You stay late. You don't want to be "difficult." You don't want to be "too much."

And then you're exhausted… and quietly resentful.

Not because you're weak.

Because somewhere along the way, your nervous system learned: *my needs cost me.*

So you stay safe by giving.

How it shows up:

- Rejection feels catastrophic.
- Boundaries feel selfish.
- Rest feels undeserved.
- Asking feels risky.

[2] Scoreboard (Comparison Trap)

Someone hits a milestone—new house, promotion, praise—and you congratulate them. You mean it.

Then later, when you're alone, it hits.

Your chest tightens. Your brain starts calculating.

Am I behind? Do I measure up? What if I never catch up?

So you push harder. You over-polish. You chase the next win.

Not because you love achievement.

Because your nervous system learned that safety lies in performance.

How it shows up:

- Validation becomes oxygen.
- You keep moving the finish line.
- You swing between perfectionism and avoidance.
- Other people's wins sting, even when you're happy for them.

[3] Scanner Mode (On Guard)

You walk into a room, and your body's already collecting data.

Who made eye contact? Who didn't?

Tone. Timing. Silence. Micro-shifts.

You get left off a thread or a meeting invite, and your body doesn't treat it like logistics. It treats it like a threat.

So you go cold—Whatever, I don't care.

Or you spiral—What did I do? Who's replacing me?

Not because you're needy.

Because connection used to be unpredictable.

So your system stays on guard.

How it shows up:

- Being left out feels like a threat.
- You assume disappointment is coming.
- You keep relationships shallow "to stay safe."
- You micromanage for certainty—or detach to avoid hurt.

These patterns often look like strengths: reliability, ambition, and independence. Until they start costing you.

THINK: YOUR RESET BUTTON (WHEN YOUR CHILDHOOD WALKS INTO THE ROOM)

You can't heal what you can't see. You also can't think your way out of wiring built through repetition.

That's why insight isn't enough.

Practice is how cycles break. Not once—over and over.

Reps build wiring.

Here's THINK for the moments your old code tries to run the meeting.

T—Track

Catch the moment your reaction is bigger than the moment.

Ask:

- What happened?

- What story did my brain write?
- Where did I feel it in my body?
- What is this reminding me of?

David's pattern became obvious: other people's wins triggered *his feeling of not being picked.*

H—Halt

Buy 10 seconds before the autopilot takes the wheel.

Exhale longer than you inhale. Drop your shoulders.

Then name it plainly: **This is shame. This is fear. This is old.**

That naming isn't fluff. Labeling emotion can help recruit regulatory control networks and reduce raw reactivity. It doesn't erase the feeling—but it changes who's driving.

I—Investigate

Be a detective, not a defendant.

Ask yourself:

- *Is this about now or then?*
- *What am I afraid will happen?*
- *What old rule is running me?*
- *What else could be true?*

Short questions. No self-trial.

N—Nurture

Steer the moment instead of being driven by it.

At work:

- "I want to respond thoughtfully. I'm going to digest and circle back."
- "Can you be specific about what 'good' looks like here?"

At home:

- "I'm getting activated. Give me ten minutes so I don't take this out on you."
- "This matters. Let's talk when I'm steady."

This teaches your nervous system: *I can stay connected without self-abandoning.*

K—Keep practicing

Progress is not "never triggered." Progress is, "I catch it sooner, and I recover faster."

You don't need to be perfect. You need reps.

Every time you pause instead of react: 1 rep.

Every time you name it instead of becoming it: 1 rep.

Every time you repair after a miss: 1 rep.

That's how the brain updates.

MAYA ANGELOU: WHEN SILENCE BECOMES VOICE

Maya Angelou knew about carrying invisible wounds. Born Marguerite Annie Johnson in 1928 in St. Louis, she experienced severe trauma at 7 years old and stopped speaking for years.

Why am I telling you about her? Because she shows what's possible when your past is loud… and you refuse to let it be the narrator.

Most of us don't go silent for years. But a lot of us go silent in other ways.

We swallow the truth. We perform "fine." We keep it moving.

We stay productive so we don't have to feel.

That's still silence. It just wears better clothes.

Maya Angelou didn't just survive trauma. She learned how it lived inside her: how it shaped her voice, her relationships, and her sense of safety in the world. And instead of letting that wound ruin her life, she used something deceptively simple to rebuild: language.

Here's THINK in real life without the perfect movie ending.

Track: Maya Angelou noticed the pattern. Silence wasn't random. It was protection.

Halt: She didn't force herself to perform on command. She created distance from what flooded her. She slowed the spiral instead of feeding it.

Investigate: She explored meaning. Not just what happened, but what it made her believe about herself.

Nurture: She used books, mentors, and creative expression to build safety and connection—one honest sentence at a time.

Keep practicing: Writing wasn't a magic eraser. It was reps. Paper after paper. Year after year.

Research suggests that naming feelings and writing them down can help the brain calm and organize emotion over time. Not overnight. Not for everyone. But it can make a difference.

You don't have to erase what happened to be free.

You just have to stop letting it speak for you.

WHAT REWIRING LOOKS LIKE

Rewiring doesn't look like a lightning bolt. It looks like the pause is showing up earlier. For David, progress wasn't "never reacting." It was catching it earlier.

At first, he'd snap, then realize two hours later.

Then 20 minutes later.

Then mid-conversation.

Then, before the words left his mouth.

That's neuroplasticity in the wild: the pause gets wider.

David built a simple protocol:

- "This is the Scoreboard. This is old."
- Long exhale
- "What am I actually afraid of?"
- One clean sentence instead of a reaction

- And when he missed repair ("I snapped. That's on me. Can we restart?")

Over time, his nervous system learned new associations:

- Someone else's win isn't my loss
- Feedback isn't shame
- Discomfort isn't danger
- A Connection can survive tension

That didn't just change him at home. It changed how he led.

Less proving. More presence.

Less defensiveness. More clarity.

Less control. More trust.

YOUR NEW BEGINNING

I can't promise you'll completely become trigger-free. That's toxic positivity bullshit. But I can promise this:

If you do this work consistently, something shifts

You catch yourself sooner. You recover faster.

You stop mistaking old fear for current truth.

You stop letting decades-old pain make today's decisions.

At first, the wins are quiet:

- a pause where you used to snap
- a boundary where you used to people-please

- a repair where you used to disappear

Then one day, you realize something bigger:

The trigger still shows up… but it doesn't get to drive.

That's freedom. Not freedom from emotion.

Freedom from running on autopilot.

Freedom to respond like the adult you are—

not the kid who had to survive.

One rep at a time.

BRAIN NOTES: THE WIRING BENEATH YOUR PATTERNS

The Family Blueprint Effect: Early family experiences create neuronal signatures that influence every relationship, personal and professional. These patterns show up in how you handle authority, conflict, and collaboration.

Neuronal Grooves: Repeated emotional experiences carve pathways that become your default responses. Understanding these patterns is the first step to changing them.

Epigenetics in Action: Childhood experiences literally change your gene expression, affecting how you respond to stress, criticism, and connection throughout your life.

The Workplace Connection: Your family patterns don't stay at home; they influence how you interact with colleagues, handle feedback, and navigate office dynamics.

The Bias Factor: Every unconscious bias stems from past experiences. Awareness of your triggers helps you respond more objectively to people and situations.

The Ripple Effect: Healing your relationship with yourself transforms all your relationships—from intimate partnerships to professional collaborations.

CHAPTER 11
THINK IN ACTION –
LEADERSHIP

UNCONSCIOUS BIAS: BREAKING THE INVISIBLE CHAINS

The meetings weren't hostile. That would've been easier.

They were polite. Professional. Smiling on the surface. And still, Donald kept leaving the room feeling smaller than when he walked in.

He'd offer an idea. John would nod, glance down, and keep the meeting moving.

"Let's circle back."

No friction. No conflict. Just... air.

Then, minutes later, Kyle would say something close enough to make Donald's jaw tighten. John would perk up. *Exactly. Great thinking, Kyle.*

At first, Donald tried to explain it away. That's what you do when something feels off but you don't have proof.

Maybe I'm reading into it.

Maybe I didn't say it clearly.

Maybe it wasn't the right moment.

So he did what high-achievers do when the rules feel slippery.

He overprepared. Overexplained. Overcorrected. He became hyper-aware of his delivery—tone, pace, phrasing—like his nervous system was constantly scanning for a mistake he couldn't see coming.

Then Elise said something in the breakroom that made the pattern undeniable.

"John told me he almost didn't hire you," she said. Casual. Like she was commenting on the coffee. "He said you have a huge accent and you'd struggle with clients." She paused. "I don't hear an accent. I don't know what he means."

Donald felt his stomach drop.

His parents were Asian. But he was born here. Raised here. English was his first language. He'd built the résumé, earned the degree, nailed the interview, and delivered results.

And still, he was being treated like a risk.

What hit hardest wasn't only the assumption. It was how the assumption came dressed as "reasonable business judgment."

Client-facing fit. Communication risk. Executive presence.

Clean language. Sharp consequences.

Donald didn't confront John. Elise didn't confront John. John didn't change.

And that's how unconscious bias survives in organizations—not through loud discrimination, but through quiet patterns people adapt to.

The Triangle of Silence

Donald absorbs it and starts editing himself.

Elise notices it and freezes—because speaking up feels risky.

John believes he's being objective, unaware his brain is running an old script.

That night, Donald replayed months of interactions through this new lens. The presentations were where John insisted on "reviewing" his client-facing materials, while no one else's were scrutinized. The meetings were where his ideas floated unacknowledged until restated by others. The subtle exclusions from key client interactions—"We need to keep the room small"—while peers with less expertise were included.

Most haunting was his own silence. Raised to believe hard work speaks for itself—to never complain and to prove his worth through results rather than confrontation—Donald had swallowed these moments one by one. Each silent accommodation had carved a neural pathway of acceptance until challenge felt impossible.

You've been there, haven't you? That moment when you finally see the pattern that's been hiding in plain sight all along. The sickening realization that what you've been feeling wasn't paranoia, but instead your intuition screaming at you while you talked yourself out of listening.

That's why silence is so costly—because the room starts to treat the bias like it's *"just how it is."*

This triangle of silence—where bias operates unchallenged, bystanders observe without intervening, and those affected accommodate rather than disrupt—represents the invisible chains that limit human potential in organizations everywhere.

YOUR BRAIN IS RUNNING A PROGRAM YOU DIDN'T WRITE

Here's what I need you to understand before we go further:

This isn't a chapter about bad people. It's a chapter about how our brains work.

Your brain is processing roughly 11 million bits of information per second. Your conscious mind? Can handle about 40 to 50.

That gap—11 million in, 40 to 50 processed—is where bias lives.

To survive that flood, your brain builds shortcuts. Fast rules. Categories. It has to. But those shortcuts were built from your history—your culture, your media, your experiences—not from the person standing in front of you right now.

Three neurological mechanisms make this especially hard to catch:

[1] The Efficiency Trap

Under pressure, your brain reaches for what's familiar: habits, stereotypes, and a "gut fee.." It builds fast rules like:

- *People who sound like me are easier with clients.*
- *She's quiet—she must not be leadership material.*
- *He talks fast and confidently—he must know what he's doing.*

Those shortcuts are efficient. They're also dangerous when it comes to people's decisions—who gets heard, who gets promoted, and who gets trusted.

John doesn't sit down and say to himself, *I'm going to be biased today.* His brain quietly runs:

Asian face + imagined accent → client risk → extra scrutiny → fewer opportunities.

Each time that pattern runs, it feels more "normal" inside his head and inside the team.

[2] The Confirmation Filter

Once your brain forms an association—like *Donald has too much of an accent*—it puts on invisible glasses that only let in evidence that supports that story:

- If Donald stumbles on one phrase: *See? Accent.*
- If he nails a presentation: *Well, that was a friendly audience.*
- If a client compliments him, they're *just being polite.*

Contradicting data gets explained away or never noticed. The loop feeds itself—quietly, automatically, convincingly.

[3] The Contagion Effect

People watch leaders to learn "how we do things here."

If a leader consistently dismisses one person's ideas and praises another's, the room learns:

- Whose voice matters
- Who it's safe to copy
- Who it's safe to ignore

Over time, that pattern spreads. Bystanders' brains mirror what they see and wire it in as "normal." That's why Elise can *know* something is wrong and still stay mostly quiet. Her brain has learned that speaking up is not *how things are done here.*

Silence teaches silence. Fairness teaches fairness.

Bias is a neural process, not a moral stain. That doesn't excuse it—it gives us leverage. The same brain that built these shortcuts can build better ones.

That's where THINK comes in.

THINK: A DEBIASING SKILL, NOT A PERSONALITY TEST

T—Track Your Thoughts

The Inner Replay

Think about a coach reviewing game film after a match. They're not watching to beat themselves up—they're watching to *see what they couldn't see at the moment*. Patterns. Habits. Blind spots.

That's what tracking your thoughts does for your leadership.

Most of us are running on a script we've never questioned—reacting to people based on old associations, old stories, and old wiring. Tracking means you start reviewing that script. Deliberately. Regularly.

Leadership Application:

- Keep a 2-minute post-meeting "bias log"—jot your immediate reactions to team members from different backgrounds. No judgment, just data.
- Before performance reviews, write down your assumptions about each employee *before* you look at their numbers.
- Track patterns in who you naturally mentor versus formally manage.
- Notice which voices you amplify in meetings—and whose contributions you tend to overlook.
- Pay attention when you describe the same behavior

differently depending on who's doing it. *(e.g., "passionate" vs. "emotional," "Confident" vs. "aggressive.")*

Why It Works:

You know that moment when you realize you've been unfair to someone—but only *hours* after the interaction? That's because awareness typically comes after the fact.

Tracking pulls it *into* the moment. It activates your prefrontal cortex—the part of your brain responsible for conscious decision-making—so you can catch a biased thought before it becomes a biased action.

When you document your thought patterns, you create distance between your automatic reactions and your leadership choices. And in that space, real change becomes possible.

H—Halt Negative Patterns

The Speed Bump Before the Reflex

In Chapter 6, you learned how to interrupt spirals in your own mind. Here, we're interrupting biased reflexes in your leadership.

Bias is like an electrical current—it takes the path of least resistance. Without interruption, it automatically follows established pathways regardless of where they lead.

You know that feeling when you catch yourself making the same mistake again? Your brain is following its familiar route. Halting means deliberately putting a speed bump in front of that reflex—so your values can catch up before your mouth opens.

Leadership Application:

- Use a "seven-second pause" before responding to ideas in meetings.
- Set your criteria *first*—before you look at resumes, rate performance, or assign promotions.
- Where possible, review written work or project proposals *without names attached*—at least once.
- Make these phrases normal in your team culture:
    - "Let's slow down one beat."
    - "Whose voice haven't we heard?"
    - "I might be missing something—someone poke holes here."

Why It Works:

Your brain has two main modes:

- Fast, automatic, emotional
- Slower, deliberate, analytical

Bias lives in the fast lane. A tiny pause—seven seconds, one slow breath—forces your brain into the slower lane, where you can remember the criteria you set, revisit your first impression, and leave space for other voices.

You're not becoming robotic. You're putting a speed bump in front of your reflex so your values can catch up.

Studies show that even a 7-second delay between stimulus and response significantly reduces bias by engaging different neural networks. These aren't magic tricks—they create the critical space where real leadership choice becomes possible.

I—Investigate Your Thoughts

Asking "Why" Until You Hit the Real Answer

In Chapter 7, you learned to be a thought detective—to keep asking *"why"* until you hit bedrock: the real fear, need, or story underneath. We're using the same tool here, just pointing at your leadership judgments.

Your biases didn't come from nowhere. They accumulated over years through media, culture, family, and experience. You didn't choose them. But they're sitting there, quietly shaping what you see and who you trust.

Investigation means shining a light on them. Not to shame yourself —to *understand* yourself. Because you can't change what you can't see.

Leadership Application:

- Take one strong "gut call" and run a **5 Whys** on it:
  - *Why do I think Donald isn't "client-ready"? → "His communication might not land."*
  - *Why? → "Clients might judge him."*
  - *Why? → "Because of his accent."*
  - *Why does that concern me? → "In a past role, a client once complained about an accent."*

- *Why does that one experience define this decision?* → *"I never questioned it."*
    - Keep going until you hit something real, something coachable, or until you realize the "reason" is just an old story wearing a professional costume.
- Compare your standards across people:
    - *Would I call this "not polished" if he looked like me?*
    - *Would I say she's "not leadership material" if she spoke with his delivery?*
- Look at patterns, not one-offs:
    - Who consistently gets stretch assignments?
    - Who always gets the invisible labor—cleanup, documentation, the work no one sees or claps for?
- Notice where your language shifts across team members: concise and positive for some, vague and cautious for others.

Why It Works:

Asking "why" again and again reveals the bedrock—the old memory or belief driving a big reaction to a small moment.

Instead of telling yourself, *I just know who's ready,* you shine a light on the story underneath that knowing. You separate behavior from bias. You decide what belongs in your future leadership—and which old beliefs need to be retired.

The discomfort you feel doing this work? It comes from the gap between how you see yourself and how you're actually showing up. Investigation bridges that gap—not to punish you, but to give you real choices.

Marcus Aurelius journaled nightly about his judgments and what he could control. If the man running an empire needed a daily bias check, so do we.

N—Nurture New Perspectives

Adding New Roads to Your Mental Map

If you always drive the same route, it's because your brain keeps sending you there. It's familiar. It's fast. It feels right.

But "familiar" isn't always accurate.

Your brain builds its understanding of people based on who you've spent time with, what you've been exposed to, and what you've been taught to notice. If that map was built in a narrow lane—same backgrounds, same experiences, same rooms—it will keep sending you to the same conclusions.

Nurturing new perspectives means deliberately adding new roads to that map.

Leadership Application:

- Try **reverse mentoring**: invite someone more junior or from a different background to mentor *you* on how they experience your team, your processes, and your communication.
- Before big decisions, make contrary perspectives a requirement:
  - *Whose lived experience would see a risk here that I'm missing?*

- *Who will this decision impact most—and who isn't in this room yet?*
- Run quick perspective-taking checks:
  - *If I grew up where she grew up, how might this feedback land?*
  - *If I were the only person of my background in this organization, how would this promotion decision feel?*
- Build mixed teams for complex work—instead of defaulting to *people like me who are easy to work with.*

Why It Works:

Think about that moment when someone explained a situation in a way that made everything suddenly click. That's your mental map updating in real time.

Perspective-taking activates networks tied to empathy and cognitive flexibility—the ability to hold more than one truth at once. Each time you intentionally seek a different view, you add a new road to your brain's map and weaken the old one that said, *My default view is the view.*

Over time, your "gut" starts including more people by default—because your map finally matches the terrain.

K—Keep Practicing

Inclusive Leadership Is a Workout, Not a Workshop

Stop expecting one training, one seminar, one book—even this one—to undo decades of wiring.

Inclusive leadership isn't a checkbox. It's a practice. Like physical fitness, it requires consistency over intensity. You don't go to the gym once and call yourself fit. You don't attend one bias training and call yourself done.

Leadership Application:

- Schedule weekly "bias workout" sessions to review decisions through an inclusion lens.
- Create accountability partnerships where colleagues check each other's thinking patterns—no judgment, just honest mirrors.
- Establish team rituals that reinforce perspective-seeking.
- Build organizational systems that reward inclusive *thinking* —not just inclusive *talking*.
- Institute regular "leadership learning loops" where you review and refine your practices over time.

Why It Works:

Think about learning to drive. At first, everything took focus: mirrors, pedals, and signs. Now you do most of it on autopilot.

That's neuroplasticity. Repetition over intensity.

Each time you:

- Track instead of defaulting
- Halt instead of reacting
- Investigate instead of defending
- Nurture a new frame instead of clinging to the old one

… you lay one more strand of myelin on the pathway of inclusive leadership. With reps, that path becomes faster and easier than the old one.

That's when you know the work is sticking: when fair, thoughtful decisions feel *natural*—not exhausting.

Practice wires the brain. Reps create the new default.

THE LEADERSHIP IMPERATIVE: BEYOND AWARENESS TO ACTION

Stories like Donald's don't have a neat resolution.

Because in reality, they rarely do.

We don't know if John ever examined his assumptions. If Elise found the courage to speak up differently next time. If Donald ever addressed what happened beyond the conversations he had with himself.

What we do know—because research shows it, and because we see it in organizations everywhere—is this:

When no one does the inner work, the outer environment doesn't change.

The invisible dynamics continue. The cycle perpetuates. And it shows up in performance data, in attrition numbers, and in the quiet erosion of trust that no engagement survey fully captures. But here's what else we know:

The brain is not fixed. Patterns are not permanent. Cultures can shift.

Not through mandates. Not through shame.

Through people—leaders and team members alike—doing the small, unglamorous, daily work of noticing, pausing, questioning, and choosing differently.

Every one of them is mid-story—not finished, not fixed. The brain that got them here can get them somewhere better. And awareness is the turning point where the story changes.

If you've been in Donald's seat:

Your exhaustion is not a weakness. Your awareness is not paranoia. The mental tax you've been paying is real—and it costs you cognitive bandwidth that should be going toward your best work.

You deserve rooms where your ideas land on their own merit. And while you work to find or build those rooms—the inner work of knowing your own worth, tracking your own patterns, and refusing to let the environment become your self-concept—that's not small.

That's foundational.

That's your invisible win.

If you've been in John's seat:

You don't have to be a bad person to have done harm through your blind spots.

But you do have to be willing to look.

The courage it takes to examine your own wiring—to sit with the discomfort of *maybe I've been getting this wrong*—is one of the most powerful things a leader can do.

Not just for the people in the room.

For who you become in the process.

If you've been in Elise's seat:

Silence feels safe in the moment.

But silence has a cost too—to the culture, to the person being harmed, and to your own nervous system, which knows what it witnessed.

One small act of courage—a question, a redirect, a "that didn't land right"—is not heroism.

It's just the next right thing.

Your brain is simultaneously the source of these shortcuts and the solution to them.

The same neuroplasticity that carved the old patterns can build new ones.

The brain that built those patterns can build better ones. Not someday. Not after the next training. Now—with every meeting you walk into, every hire you make, and every moment you choose to pause instead of default.

You didn't choose the previous old wiring. But you get to choose what happens next.

The question was never, *Do I have bias?*

You do. I do. We all do.

The real question—the one worth sitting with long after you close this chapter—is *What am I willing to do with that knowledge in my next meeting, my next hire, and my next conversation?*

Because the people in your rooms are already paying the price for unchecked shortcuts. *Inclusion requires deliberate rewiring.*

And you—right now, with this awareness—have the capacity to change that.

Not by being perfect. By being willing.

Willing to track. To halt. To investigate. To nurture. To keep practicing.

That's not a small ask. But it's also not an impossible one.

It's the next right move. In the next room. With the next person.

That's where invisible wins are made. And you are more ready than you think.

CHAPTER 12
THINK IN ACTION – BURNOUT

THE SLOW BOIL: WHEN WORK BECOMES SURVIVAL

2:03 a.m.

Highway lights smear into white lines. Jimmy's eyes fight to stay open. This is his third near miss of the night. The guardrail gets too close, like it's reaching for him.

His body had been sending up flares for months.

Hey, Jimmy. Something's off. Listen.

He'd learned to treat them like spam.

He would treat them like glitches. Like inconveniences.

They're not.

They're messages.

Jimmy didn't wake up one day "burned out."

He boiled slowly.

At first, the job felt like proof: *I made it.*

Validation that the years of sacrifice had meant something.

Prestigious bank. Great title. Big future.

Then the dream started rearranging his life. Quietly. Daily. One compromise at a time—until he couldn't tell whether he chose it... or it chose for him.

Maybe you've been there too. Chasing the promotion, the title, the income so hard you couldn't tell anymore if you were driving the dream or the dream was driving you.

And then there was **Matt.**

Matt could turn the phrase "team player" into a leash.

"Need team players here," he'd say—while assigning a 400-profile data entry task at 6:42 p.m.

His favorite Teams message: ***"Quick meeting?"***

Translation: "*Cancel your evening.*"

Matt never rolled up his sleeves. Never stayed late to help—only to watch. He measured loyalty by face time. Nobody left before him. It wasn't written anywhere. It didn't need to be.

Chances are you've met Matt.

The kind of leader who confuses delegation with leadership. Urgency with importance. Control with excellence.

If Jimmy had paused to ask, *Is this about the work—or the power?* He might have seen the trap sooner. But asking it out loud would have cost him his job. So he stayed quiet. So did all his teammates.

Fourteen-hour days. A two-hour commute each way. Three hours of sleep on a good night. Coffee that stopped working.

Weight creeping on. Salt, sugar, crunch. His brain was hunting for the quickest dopamine hit it could find.

And here's the part people get wrong:

His body wasn't failing him. It was trying to save him.

Cravings, exhaustion, and weight gain: these aren't moral issues. They're desperate adaptations from a nervous system stuck in survival.

This is **hedonic adaptation**. Our brain is physiologically adjusting to conditions that were never sustainable. In a modern workplace, it's how we normalize our own slow collapse.

His brain adjusted to a reality that was never okay, what researchers call **normalization of deviance.** The change is gradual. The tolerance builds. The smoke detector gets quieter. Until the phrase *"this isn't normal"* doesn't even occur to you anymore.

You used to leave at 6:30 p.m., feeling vaguely guilty about unanswered emails. Now you check Slack at midnight and feel *productive.*

It's death by a thousand tiny compromises—each one justifiably reasonable in the moment.

The promotion was always "next quarter." The finish line kept moving. And Jimmy kept running—because stopping meant admitting that all those stolen dinners and missed weekends had been for nothing. *I've already sacrificed so much; I can't quit now.* What if the real question isn't *can I afford to leave?* but *can I afford to stay?*

Around him, the evidence was everywhere. Sarah, who used to light up talking about her kid's soccer goals, now stared blankly at her screen. Mike looked genuinely confused when someone asked what he did for fun—as if he'd misplaced the concept entirely. Jimmy's wife still left his dinner plate on the counter. Always cold. The stack of plastic-wrapped plates in the fridge became a quiet monument to everything the job had taken.

When you're running on static, you can't think your way out. You just keep moving because stopping requires energy you don't have.

That's not weakness. That's what a system looks like when it's been run past empty.

YOUR BRAIN ON BURNOUT

Burnout is not just really bad stress.

A **stressor** is the external trigger: the impossible deadline, the boss who messages at 10 p.m., or the commute that steals two hours of your day. **Stress** is your internal neurological response—the cortisol spike, the adrenaline surge, and the narrowed focus. You can't always control the stressor. But understanding your stress response is where your power lives.

Here's how stress and burnout differ in real life:

	Stress	Burnout
Duration	Acute. Resolves when the stressor passes	Chronic. Builds slowly, doesn't resolve on its own
Scope	Tied to one project, deadline, or situation	Spills into everything, even work you used to enjoy
Recovery	Rest helps; you bounce back	Rest doesn't fix it; you're still exhausted
Emotion	Tense, wired, urgent	Empty, flat, cynical, detached
Performance	May fuel a final push	Makes even simple tasks feel impossible

Stress is your brain doing its job—your cortisol spikes, focus narrows, and the threat response activates. In short doses with real recovery, it can sharpen your focus. The problem is when the stressors never let up. When the "on" switch gets stuck. When a system built for sprints is forced to run a marathon with no finish line.

Researchers call this **allostatic overload**—the cumulative breakdown when your stress architecture has been running in overdrive so long it can no longer return to baseline. Burnout isn't just a feeling. It rewires how your brain functions.

Here's what that looks like—in three specific, recognizable ways.

[1] Exhaustion—The Drained Tank

Burnout exhaustion is not ordinary tiredness. Sleep doesn't fix it. A long weekend doesn't touch it. Your HPA axis—the system responsible for cortisol regulation—has been dysregulated by sustained overload. The brain, starved of real recovery, starts hunting for the fastest fuel it can find: sugar, salt, fat, caffeine. You're not weak. You're a system running on empty, doing what depleted systems do.

Does this sound like you? You read the same email three times and still can't absorb it. You open your laptop and stare at something you've done hundreds of times—and can't begin. The thought of one more hour "on" makes you want to disappear. You're not lazy. You're depleted in ways that rest hasn't been allowed to touch.

[2] Cynicism & Detachment—The Emotional Numbing

Cynicism isn't an attitude problem. It's a protective shutdown.

When chronic stress keeps the amygdala in a constant state of activation, the brain pulls resources away from emotional engagement. Your dopamine and serotonin systems—which make work feel meaningful and relationships feel rewarding—get chronically suppressed. The reward signal goes quiet. What remains feels hollow.

You used to care. You *remember* caring. Now you're going through the motions—performing the version of you that used to show up. The dark jokes multiply. The eye rolls happen before the meeting starts.

Recognize this? You sit through the all-hands with your camera off, not because you have nothing to say, but because *what's the point?* You've shared ideas before—watched them absorbed without credit, restated by someone else, lauded. So you stop. The silence isn't disengagement. It's self-protection.

[3] Reduced Professional Efficacy—The Shrinking Wins

This is the hardest to name—because it feels like failure.

You know what you're capable of. But the work that used to flow—decisions, creativity, execution—now takes twice as long and still doesn't feel right. Small errors creep in. You're trying just as hard. It just isn't showing up.

This is not incompetence. This is how your brain is wired.

Under sustained cortisol elevation, the prefrontal cortex—your brain's planning and decision-making center—is literally less available. The hippocampus, which consolidates memory and learning, is impaired. You're working with a compromised system, and the harder you push, the wider the gap between effort and output.

Does this sound like you? You triple-check emails before sending. You avoid complex projects because you don't trust yourself to finish them well. You feel behind before you start. You used to love a challenge—now you're afraid of it.

> **A gentle note:** Burnout and depression can look similar—and they can co-exist. If low mood, loss of joy, or persistent hopelessness is bleeding into *most* areas of your life beyond

work, please talk to a professional. You don't have to figure this out alone.

THINK IN ACTION

This is where we move from *knowing* to *doing*. When burnout is in the room, THINK becomes your intervention tool.

T—Track Your Thoughts | *The Burnout Detector*

When you're burned out, your brain can't accurately assess itself. The regions responsible for self-awareness are among the first casualties of chronic stress. You adapt to the unbearable so completely that it stops feeling unbearable—it just feels *like your life*.

Burnout Application:

- Keep a "depletion diary"—note when routine tasks feel unreasonably hard.
- Track physical signals: disrupted sleep, appetite shifts, tension headaches, and brain fog.
- Document "emotion mismatch" moments—when your reaction is bigger than the situation warrants.
- Watch for "time distortion"—when hours blur and you can't account for your day.

Why it works: An external record creates the distance your exhausted brain can't manufacture on its own. It's like a trusted friend saying, "Hey—I've noticed something. This hasn't been okay for a while." That outside perspective breaks through the normalization of suffering that makes burnout so quietly devastating.

Made visible, patterns become choices. Hidden, they become fate.

H—Halt Negative Patterns | *The Depletion Circuit Breaker*

Burnout has momentum. Every depleting choice—the late reply, the skipped lunch, the "just one more thing"—makes the next one easier and the next boundary softer. Without a deliberate interruption, the spiral continues until the system breaks.

Burnout Application:

- Set non-negotiable exits: *"I leave at 6 p.m.—full stop."*
- Use physical pattern breakers: alarms to stand, breathe, and drink water.
- Create communication limits: no email after 8 p.m., phone out of the bedroom.
- Build micro-recovery between demands—even five minutes of deliberate stillness resets cortisol.

Why it works: Your depleted brain cannot be trusted to know when enough is enough. Chronic stress impairs the prefrontal circuits you need for self-regulation—the very circuits required to set a limit. External circuit breakers bypass the compromised internal signal. You install the sprinkler system *before* the fire, not while you're standing in the smoke.

What if Jimmy had one non-negotiable: leave at 6 p.m., no exceptions? That one boundary, held consistently, might have slowed the spiral enough for him to see his options.

I—Investigate Your Thoughts | *The Burnout Archaeologist*

Burnout rarely starts with bad intentions. It often starts with good ones: *dedication, excellence, loyalty, and not wanting to let people down.* Investigation means tracing how those virtues became the architecture of your exhaustion.

Burnout Application:

- Where did you learn that your worth equals your output?
- Who are you still trying to prove yourself to?
- What do you fear will actually happen if you admit you're not okay?
- What do you honestly believe would happen if you said no?

Why it works: The beliefs driving burnout feel like *facts*. Investigation activates your prefrontal cortex—analytical thinking over emotional autopilot—so you can finally read the warning labels on what you've been handling without protection.

What if Jimmy had questioned whether a promotion *in this environment* would actually improve his life or just give him more access to the machine consuming him? Many of the constraints keeping him trapped were self-imposed stories, not external realities.

N—Nurture New Perspectives | *The Burnout Reframer*

Burnout doesn't just drain your energy—it narrows your vision. Problems look unsolvable. Options disappear. Hope feels naive. That tunnel vision isn't a character flaw; it's a neurological consequence of a threat-response system running the show.

Burnout Application:

- Practice "both-and" thinking: *I can be dedicated AND have limits.*
- Reframe: You are a battery, not a power plant. Batteries require recharging. That's not weakness—it's design.
- Ask: *What would I tell my closest friend if they were living my exact life right now?*
- Replace "this is the only way" with "this is one way among many."

Why it works: Chronic stress narrows attention to immediate danger—life-saving for predators, devastating for workplaces. Introducing new perspectives activates different neural networks: creativity, possibility, and problem-solving. It's switching from a flashlight to a floodlight.

What would Jimmy have told his best friend? "Stop. This job is not worth your life." Without hesitation. The cruelest part of burnout is the different standards we apply to ourselves versus everyone we love.

K—Keep Practicing | *The Recovery Athlete*

Recovery from burnout isn't a single decision. It's a practice—like athletic training after injury. Gradual, consistent, patient. The goal isn't perfection. The goal is direction.

Burnout Application:

- Establish daily non-negotiables: protected sleep, real breaks, movement, and time outside.
- Start boundary-setting in low-stakes situations—you're training new neural pathways.
- Create a "minimum viable recovery plan" for high-pressure stretches (because life doesn't pause).
- Build a relapse protocol: *When I notice [these signs], I will do [this].*

Why it works: Willpower draws from the same neural resources that burnout depletes—that's the cruel paradox. But small, consistent actions build stronger neural pathways than sporadic, intense efforts. Over time, recovery stops feeling like an act of will and starts feeling like second nature.

What if Jimmy had started with one anchor: seven hours of sleep two nights a week? One protected recovery point might have slowed the spiral just enough for clarity to return.

THE PERSONAL COST NO ONE TALKS ABOUT

Health: Chronic burnout is linked to elevated cortisol, cardiovascular risk, suppressed immune function, and increased risk of anxiety and depression. Jimmy's weight gain, his trembling hands, and his inability to stay awake—these weren't personality issues. They were physiological consequences.

Relationships: Jimmy's wife's cold dinner plates were more than a logistical problem. They were the shape of emotional absence. Burnout doesn't stay at work—it bleeds into how present you are for your kids, your partner, your friends.

Identity: When work is your primary source of self-worth—and work becomes something you dread, survive, endure—the question *Who am I without this?* becomes terrifying. Burned-out people don't just lose productivity. They lose themselves.

Career: The cruel irony is that burnout creates the conditions most likely to end the career someone burned themselves out protecting. Errors and disengagement accumulate quietly until the damage is done.

THE ORGANIZATIONAL COST LEADERS CANNOT AFFORD TO IGNORE

Gallup research shows burned-out employees are:

- **63% more likely** to take a sick day
- **2.6x as likely** to actively seek a different job
- **23% less likely** to visit the emergency room—meaning they're suppressing symptoms and showing up anyway, costing *more* in the long run

The American Institute of Stress estimates workplace stress costs U.S. employers over **$300 billion annually** in absenteeism, diminished productivity, turnover, and healthcare costs.

When Jimmy finally leaves—and burned-out employees almost always leave—the organization loses his institutional knowledge, absorbs replacement costs (estimated at 1.5 -- 2x annual salary), and restarts the cycle with someone new. If the culture that burned him out is still intact.

This is not a wellness issue. It's a performance and retention strategy.

Matt didn't set out to drive talented people out. But the culture he created—where visibility equated with value and exhaustion with loyalty—did exactly that. Leaders create culture by what they reward, what they tolerate, and what they model. When burnout is tolerated, it is effectively endorsed.

THE BURNOUT IMPERATIVE: FROM SURVIVAL TO SUSTAINABILITY

Jimmy's story isn't exceptional. It's the rule. Burnout follows a predictable pattern—and that means it can be spotted and interrupted before collapse.

1. **Normalization of abnormal.** When Matt stayed late and expected everyone to follow, he was enforcing an unspoken standard: *visible exhaustion equals commitment.* This is cultural gaslighting—it leads people to question their own legitimate needs rather than challenge unreasonable demands. The antidote isn't a wellness program. It's leadership that models limits openly, without apology.

2. **The contamination effect.** Jimmy's work stress didn't stay at work. It depleted the very coping resources he needed to change anything. Burnout is not a contained event—it's a system-wide infection. Leaders who say "leave work at work" while sending 9 p.m. Slack messages aren't modeling containment. They're perpetuating it.

3. **The depletion spiral.** As Jimmy's resources ran dry, his ability to change his circumstances shrank. The cognitive load of overwork left no capacity for job-searching, boundary-setting, or reaching out. Burnout destroys the tools needed to escape it. **Prevention beats rescue—always.** Build the buffers before the crisis.

THE CULTURE RESET: WHAT LEADERS AND TEAMS MUST DO NOW

For leaders: this isn't about being "nice." Brains under chronic threat narrow attention, make risk-averse choices, and erode trust. When you design for recovery, autonomy, and real psychological safety, performance follows.

Practical resets:

- Protect time off like a safety protocol—because it is.
- Audit workloads before adding to them.
- Create norms where no one is rewarded for being last online.
- Coach leaders to notice depletion signals before they show up as performance problems.
- Ask your team, "What's one thing that drains your energy that doesn't have to?" Then fix it.

For teams, burnout is cultural before it's personal. Psychological safety, workload clarity, and fair distribution aren't perks. They're your productivity infrastructure.

For the men carrying the "provider" story—trained to equate silence with strength and output with worth: your family needs you *present,* not just employed. Your team needs your clear thinking—not your midnight emails. **Strength is a wise limit, held with conviction.**

THINK gives you levers at every layer—from your inner dialogue to the norms your team lives by. You don't need permission to start.

Burnout is not a character flaw. It is a predictable outcome of unsustainable systems.

Your exhaustion isn't a weakness. It's your humanity asserting itself against impossible demands.

The question was never whether you have limits. Everyone does.

The question is whether you discover them through intentional boundaries—or through collapse.

THINK helps you choose the former before the latter becomes inevitable.

CHAPTER 13
THINK IN ACTION – TOXIC WORKPLACE

WHEN THE WORKPLACE BECOMES A WAR ZONE

I was supposed to be on PTO.

But we were short-staffed. A colleague had quit, leaving months of undocumented work behind. So I volunteered to step in because I was supposed to be the "high performer." The one who could hold it all together. The one who said yes when everyone else looked away.

It was May 2021.

My mother was in the hospital awaiting kidney stone surgery. COVID meant limited visitors—just my sister and me, rotating shifts, a few days at a time. So while my mother recovered, I lived in that hospital room, bouncing between her bedside and my laptop, telling myself: *Just get through this.*

The fluorescent lights buzzed overhead. My mother lay in the bed beside me, finally asleep after a morning of pain. I had my laptop balanced on my knees, answering emails while helping nurses reposition her. Twenty-two hours without sleep and counting.

A notification flashed on Slack from my coworker, Ella.

"Khai, I need you to fix this calculation error."

The nurse appeared at the doorway with an update on my mom's surgery. I nodded, scribbling notes on a scrap of paper, phone still in my hand.

Nine minutes later, Ella messaged, *"Still waiting."*

Then, Ella messaged the entire department: *"Still dealing with quality issues Khai has produced. Will update when we can move forward."*

I hadn't even opened the file yet. And the errors she was referring to? They weren't mine. They originated from months of undocumented work my former colleague had left behind—work I had repeatedly flagged as problematic before this person's departure. Nobody listened. What Ella also didn't mention was that I was answering from a hospital room, mid-surgery update, expected to instantly untangle someone else's mess.

But what did I do? I blamed myself. A familiar knot tightened in my stomach—shame, rage, and helplessness braided together so tight I could barely breathe.

Weeks earlier, I had spoken to my manager about Ella's behavior. Her response: "She has Asperger's syndrome, and I'm sure she doesn't mean any harm. Don't take it personally. She's one of our smartest people."

222

I want to pause here—because the issue matters. Neurodivergence is real, and it deserves genuine compassion and thoughtful accommodation. But compassion for one person's neurological wiring cannot serve as a blanket permission to cause harm. Understanding *why* someone behaves a certain way is not the same as excusing the impact on others. Both things can be true: Ella may not have intended cruelty, and I was still being crushed. A leader's job is to hold both truths, not use one to erase the other.

What that response really told me was: *your pain doesn't count here.*

After that, I didn't get louder. I got smaller. Worked later. Apologized faster. Tried harder.

I watched a colleague break down in tears after a similar public dressing-down. I felt for her, but I said nothing. I had nothing left to give—not even basic human solidarity. My emotional bank account was deeply overdrawn.

The pattern continued. Each morning, I rehearsed what I would say if Ella came at me in a meeting. Each night, I lay awake replaying the day's humiliations, crafting perfect responses that came hours too late. The weight piled on—fifteen pounds in two months. My skin broke out. My reflection looked like a stranger.

But it was the emptiness in my eyes that frightened me most.

What cut deepest was my manager's silence—someone I'd expected to recognize the pattern and to stand up for me. Instead, she became complicit. The boys' club, I expected to fight. The abandonment by my own gender, I didn't.

A few days later, my shift ended at the hospital. I came home.

I wasn't even looking forward to my own bed. I sat down next to Iri —our rescued English bulldog—for no real reason, with no intention. Just because she was there and the floor was closer than anywhere else I needed to be.

I wasn't thinking about resting. I wasn't thinking about tomorrow. All I could think was: *this will all be over soon.* And for the first time in weeks, that thought felt like relief.

Then she pressed her paw into my hand.

Once. I didn't move.

Again. Then again. She wouldn't stop. She shifted her whole body closer and laid her head on my chest—heavy, warm, deliberate— like she was anchoring me to the floor on purpose.

But something about the weight of her—the repetition, the *insistence*—cracked something open in me. A thought I hadn't been able to reach in months: *Iri is choosing me. Right now. As I am. I am left with nothing else to offer.*

That was the epiphany. Not loud. Not dramatic. Just a small, quiet shift—a crack of light in a room I'd forgotten had windows.

That's when I knew I needed professional help. The next morning, I called my doctor. I had to step away from this toxic workplace.

Recovery didn't look inspirational. It looked like stillness, therapy, medication, and trial and error. And one unexpected thing: Mark Rober's creative engineering class. No deadlines. No performance reviews. Just curiosity and play. Slowly, my body softened. My mind began to breathe again.

That's when it hit me: I wasn't stupid. I wasn't weak. I wasn't broken.

I was depleted.

That's when I told myself I would never again let the toxic shit at work determine my worth. I would never again let life's injustice and feelings of drowning push me to the edge. It was the third time suicide had crossed my mind as a solution. And it was the last time. And it was the last time.

What you just read isn't about one difficult colleague. It's what a brain looks like under sustained, targeted pressure—and why "just push through" was never actually an option.

THE NEUROLOGICAL HIJACKING OF WORKPLACE TOXICITY

What makes toxic workplaces so devastating isn't just the unpleasant interactions—it's how they rewire our brains in specific ways that make escape increasingly difficult. Building on what we learned about bias in leadership and depletion in burnout, targeted toxicity introduces three additional neurological mechanisms:

[1] The Social Threat Response

Your brain processes social rejection through the same neural pathways as physical pain. When someone publicly criticizes your work, your brain registers it as a genuine threat to survival—activating the amygdala while suppressing the prefrontal cortex. In the moments you most need clarity and creativity, your brain is physiologically unavailable. Chronic social threat damages the hippocampus and shrinks the neural connections responsible for decision-making.

[2] The Contamination Effect

Toxic environments create negative neuroplasticity—your brain rewires itself to anticipate and prepare for hostility. This hypervigilance doesn't turn off when you leave work. The same neural networks activated during workplace conflict stay active at home, making you reactive to minor stressors and less present with the people you love. That's why I flinched when my partner reached for my hand. My brain had reconfigured itself for constant defense— and it didn't know how to stand down.

[3] The Identity Erosion

Prolonged exposure to toxic environments damages the brain's self-referential networks, or areas responsible for maintaining your sense of identity and worth. As these networks weaken, you become more susceptible to internalizing external criticisms. This explains why workplace toxicity doesn't just make you feel bad temporarily but can fundamentally alter how you see yourself, leading to profound identity loss like I experienced staring in the bathroom mirror.

Now that you understand what's happening inside your brain, here's what you can actually do about it—at work and at home.

THINK IN ACTION

T—Track Your Thoughts

The Toxicity Detector

In toxic environments, your perception becomes warped—what's abnormal slowly begins to seem normal. Tracking creates an objective record that helps you maintain perspective when your internal compass is compromised.

Toxic Workplace Application:

- Document specific incidents of toxic behavior with dates and details.
- Track physical symptoms that appear during or after work interactions.
- Note changes in your self-talk before, during, and after work.
- Identify the boundary that was crossed (respect, clarity, fairness, workload, dignity).
- Monitor "contamination" instances when work toxicity affects personal life.

Why It Works: Toxicity thrives in fog—confusion, self-doubt, and "maybe it's just me." Tracking forces your brain back into **reality**. It interrupts gaslighting, restores cause-and-effect, and protects identity before it erodes.

If I had logged each Ella incident—date, words, audience, and impact—I would've stopped arguing with my own reality. I would've seen the pattern: public blame, timed to moments I was already stretched thin, then dismissed by leadership as "just who she is." And I would've moved sooner—with proof in my hand, not panic in my chest.

H—Halt Negative Patterns

The Toxicity Circuit Breaker

Toxic environments create undesirable yet powerful momentum. One hostile message triggers a defensive response, which triggers another hit, and suddenly the conflict owns your whole nervous system. Halting means deliberately interrupting the cycle before it becomes your default.

Toxic Workplace Application:

- **Create physical distance when escalation starts.**
  Bathroom break, water refill, step outside—90 seconds can shift your state.
- **Delay responses to hostile messages.** If it spikes your heart rate, it doesn't deserve an instant reply.
- **Use a pattern-interrupt phrase.**
  - "I want to respond thoughtfully—give me time and I'll follow up."
  - "I'm not able to answer at this moment. I'll come back with specifics."
  - "I can deliver A and B by Friday. C will need to shift or be reassigned."

- **Set communication boundaries.** One channel, one thread, written requirements, clear deadlines.
- **Use a decontamination ritual** between work and home (2–10 minutes): change clothes, take a quick walk or shower, or do a breathing reset—something that tells your body, "We're not there anymore."
- **Develop "toxicity aliases" to maintain psychological distance.**

Alias	What It Looks Like
Public-Shame Pattern	Calling you out in group channels
Urgency Trap	"Need this now" → blame if instant compliance doesn't happen
Moving Goalposts	Standards change after you deliver
Credit Theft	Your work becomes someone else's accomplishment
Isolation Tactic	Excluding you from meetings/information that affects your work

What that means: A "toxicity alias" is a short label you give to a *recurring toxic pattern* so you can recognize it quickly without personalizing it. You're not naming the person—you're naming the move.

Examples: How to use it in real time:

1. In your head: *Alias: Moving Goalposts.*

2. Out loud, neutral: "Can we align on criteria in writing so we're working from the same definition of 'done'?"

3. Then a boundary: "Once we confirm criteria, I can deliver by ___."

Why It Works: Toxic workplaces thrive on automatic reactions. Your brain in threat mode can't access its higher functions. It's physiologically incapable of creative problem-solving or nuanced communication. Circuit breakers (distance, delay, a phrase, a ritual) create space between trigger and response, allowing your nervous system to regulate and your prefrontal cortex to come back online. It's like pressing pause on a runaway train, creating the crucial moment needed to switch tracks.

If I had paused before responding—thirty minutes, three breaths, one factual line—I would've protected my nervous system. That Slack chaos would have still followed me home, but I might've walked through the door with a little more of myself still intact.

I—Investigate Your Thoughts

The Toxicity Archaeologist

Toxic environments implant thoughts that aren't yours—criticisms, limitations, and judgments that you begin to mistake for your own voice. Investigation is how you excavate what's true, what's manipulation, and what you've been conditioned to carry.

Toxic Workplace Application:

[1] Separate facts from meaning.

- **Facts:** what was said/done, what changed, what you delivered, and what you were asked for.
- **Meaning:** what you concluded about yourself ("I'm failing," "I'm unsafe," "I'm not enough").

[2] Challenge the conclusion, not your worth.

Ask:

- "What evidence supports this meaning?"
- "What evidence does not?"
- "What else could explain this—unclear criteria, bad process, politics, or poor leadership?"

[3] Write one reality statement.

One sentence that's specific and provable:

- "The criteria changed after delivery."
- "The errors originated upstream."
- "Feedback was delivered publicly."
- "The timeline doesn't match the scope."

[4] Name what you need next.

Clarity? Criteria? Timeline? Resources? Privacy? A documented agreement?

This is where you stop begging for approval and start asking for what makes work workable.

Why It Works: Toxic workplaces succeed by making you internalize external problems and convince you that you're the issue rather than the environment. This internalization happens below conscious awareness, as your brain tries to create a sense of control in an uncontrollable situation. Investigation activates your analytical brain, helping you distinguish your authentic thoughts from implanted ones.

If I had separated facts from meaning, I would've caught the lie faster: "I'm letting the team down" was a story planted on top of someone else's errors and a broken process. Investigation would've helped me stop begging for approval and start asking for what makes work workable.

N—Nurture New Perspectives

Reclaim your options

Toxic environments don't just drain your energy—they shrink your world. They collapse your sense of what's available to you until escape feels like the only option and staying feels like the only reality. Nurture is about reclaiming what the threat response stole: your ability to see what's actually possible from here.

Your brain has been trained to see one door. This step is about remembering that the others exist.

Toxic Workplace Application:

[1] Grant yourself the grace you give freely.

Ask yourself, *What would I tell a close friend in this exact situation?* Then give yourself that same answer. Nurturing yourself means extending the same possibility-thinking to yourself that you'd freely give someone you love.

[2] Build your Options Map (one page).

Create 3 columns (Stay + Protect | Stay + Escalate | Exit + Reclaim)

Stay + Protect	Stay + Escalate	Exit + Reclaim
What boundary reduces exposure this week?	Who is one safe leader outside my chain?	What's my 30–60 day runway?
What work can be clarified, narrowed, or put in writing?	What is the cleanest formal path (HR/ethics/skip-level)?	Who can refer me?
What support do I need outside work to stay regulated?	What documentation do I already have—and what's missing?	What role would treat me like a human again?

[3] Decide on your direction for the next two weeks.

Not forever. Two weeks.

Pick one lane: protect, escalate, or exit. Commit to two small actions.

Forward motion—even one inch—restores a sense of agency that toxicity systematically dismantled.

Why It Works: Toxic environments manipulate your perception by creating artificial constraints. Your brain's threat response narrows attention to focus on immediate dangers, creating tunnel vision that prevents you from seeing escape routes or alternatives. This evolutionary adaptation, helpful when facing a predator, becomes destructive in toxic workplaces where the "danger" is often social rejection or professional consequences. Deliberately introducing new perspectives activates different neural networks associated with creativity and problem-solving. It's like switching from a flashlight to a floodlight—suddenly, the darkness that seemed impenetrable reveals paths you couldn't previously see.

If I had built an Options Map in the middle of that hospital-room season, my brain would've stopped treating survival as the only plan. I wasn't trapped—I was exhausted and isolated. Those are very different problems with very different solutions. And different problems have more doors.

K—Keep Practicing

The Toxicity Resistance Trainer

Reclaiming yourself from a toxic environment isn't a one-time decision. It requires consistent practice: building new neural pathways that can withstand the powerful pull of established toxic dynamics. Just as an athlete trains to perform under pressure, you train your brain to maintain boundaries and perspective—until protection becomes instinct.

Toxic Workplace Application:

- Practice boundary statements until they become automatic.
- Regularly implement stress recovery techniques to prevent depletion.
- Maintain an identity anchor outside work (class, art, gym, volunteering).
- Keep a weekly check-in with someone outside the system who knows the real you.
- Keep two files:

(i) Proof file (wins, praise, impact)

(ii) Values file (what you won't trade anymore)

Why It Works: Toxic environments wire you through repetition. Reclamation does too. Consistent reps turn protection from exhausting effort into automatic self-respect—so your nervous system stops living at the mercy of someone else's mood.

If I had practiced one boundary sentence a day, plus a five-minute recovery ritual after each hit, I would've rebuilt self-trust sooner while I was still inside the system. Weekly contact with someone outside the workplace could've anchored me when my perspective wavered. Small reps. Consistent. That's how resistance stops being exhausting—and becomes automatic.

THE WORKPLACE TOXICITY IMPERATIVE: FROM SURVIVAL TO RECLAMATION

Christine Porath's decades of research on workplace incivility confirm what neuroscience already shows: the cost of toxic cultures isn't just human—it's organizational. Disengagement, turnover, lost innovation, and eroded trust are measurable outcomes. The question isn't whether your organization can afford to address this. It's whether it can afford not to.

Three patterns create the conditions for toxicity to take root:

[1] Weaponized vulnerability

When someone is caregiving, grieving, sick, or stretched thin—and the workplace responds with pressure or public blame—vulnerability becomes a weapon.

A sustainable approach recognizes that vulnerability isn't an exception—it's part of being human. And humanity shows up differently. Some team members process the world differently, communicate differently, and need different structures to do their best work. Designing for psychological safety means designing for *all* of that—not just the loudest voices or the most familiar styles. Inclusion isn't a checkbox. It's the architecture of a team where everyone can actually function.

[2] The bystander effect

Toxicity isn't only the aggressor. It's the room that stays silent. Silence isn't neutral. Silence teaches one lesson: **this is allowed here.**

236

A healthier culture makes intervention normal through clear norms, safe reporting, and real consequences for public humiliation.

[3] Identity theft

The endgame of unchecked toxicity is erosion: people stop trusting themselves, stop recognizing themselves, and start negotiating their worth away—quietly, invisibly, until they're gone. A preemptive approach protects identity through clarity, dignity, and accountability—so people don't have to shrink to survive.

YOU WERE NEVER THE PROBLEM

Workplace toxicity isn't a reflection of your worth. It's a dysfunction of a system. Your suffering isn't weakness—it's your humanity responding to an inhuman environment.

Recovery doesn't always look the way we expect. It doesn't always feel like a comeback. Sometimes it looks like calling your doctor on a Monday morning. Like sitting still long enough to breathe. Like building a ridiculous dog-treat launcher in a creative engineering class just to remember what it feels like to be curious again. Like letting a rescued English bulldog press herself against your legs until the shaking stops.

You weren't broken. You were depleted. Those are very different things—and that distinction matters.

You don't need to win the whole war this week. You need one reclaimed inch of ground—one boundary, one ally, one log entry, one decision that says: *I'm still here. And I'm not available for erasure.*

And for the leader reading this: if you've ever brushed off someone's complaint as "that's just how they are," I'm not here to shame you. I'm here to offer you a different lens. What you said in that moment—however unintentionally—was: the system matters more than the human. And that belief is how harm becomes culture.

You have the power to change that. Not by being perfect, but by being willing to look.

No job is worth the sacrifice of your fundamental selfhood.

MY NOTES FOR THE READERS: WHY THIS WORK MATTERS

This chapter is heavy—intentionally. Because what I've described isn't rare.

In the year after I returned to work, 3 men and 1 woman in my local community took their own lives. People said the same things about all of them: "strong," "reliable," "fine." We didn't see it coming. We never do—until it's too late.

This isn't only unfolding in toxic workplaces. It's unfolding in backyards and at dining tables. In the quiet hours after the kids are in bed. In the car before walking through the front door. In the minds of people who show up every single day and say nothing.

That's why I wrote this chapter. That's why I do this work. Not to point fingers. Not to assign blame. But because the invisible battles are real—and they deserve to be seen.

If this chapter found you at your lowest, I want you to know: you are not alone. And your life is not up for debate.

If you or someone you know is struggling, please reach out to the 988 Suicide and Crisis Lifeline by calling or texting 988.

PART FIVE
BEYOND THE INDIVIDUAL

CHAPTER 14
THE RIPPLE EFFECT
STARTS WITH YOU

HOW YOUR SMALLEST MOMENTS CREATE THE BIGGEST CHANGES

Here's a question that might change everything: What if the way you show up in the tiniest moments—how you breathe when your kid is melting down, the tone you use when someone cuts you off in traffic, the energy you bring when you walk through your front door—could literally change the world around you?

Not in some mystical way. In a real, measurable, neuroscientific way.

Your brain doesn't exist in isolation. Every time you interact with another person, your nervous systems are having a conversation.

Your emotional state becomes the weather for everyone in your orbit.

So—what kind of weather are you creating?

EMOTIONAL CONTAGION: THE RIPPLE YOU DIDN'T REALIZE YOU WERE SENDING

Emotional contagion isn't a personality trait. It's a human feature.

When you walk into a room and you're tense, people don't just *notice* it. Their bodies respond—heart rate climbs, breathing gets shallow, and stress rises—often without conscious awareness.

And it works in reverse, too. When you walk in calm and centered, the people around you begin to mirror that state. Their nervous systems soften. Thinking clears. It feels safer to be human.

Dr. Elaine Hatfield's research suggests emotional contagion happens through three primary mechanisms:

1. **Automatic Mimicry:** Your facial muscles unconsciously mirror the expressions around you. When you mimic a smile, it can activate the same neural pathways as genuine happiness.

2. **Convergence:** Your breathing, heart rate, and physiological rhythms begin to synchronize with the people you're interacting with.

3. **Contagion:** Over time, those shared signals create a shared emotional state. Stress spreads. Calm spreads. Irritation spreads. Safety spreads.

This is why influence is happening even when you're not "trying to lead."

It's what people feel when they're around you—because your nervous system is always in conversation with theirs.

WHY BIG CHANGES FEEL IMPOSSIBLE (AND WHAT ACTUALLY WORKS)

Let's be honest about something: you've probably tried to change before. Maybe you decided to be more patient with your family. Or less reactive at work. Or kinder to strangers. You had good intentions and real motivation, and for a few days or weeks, you felt like you were making progress

Then life happened. Stress hit. You got tired. And suddenly you were right back where you started, maybe feeling even worse about yourself than before.

Here's what I want you to know:

You're not broken. You're not weak. Your brain is working exactly as it's designed to.

When you try to make big changes, your brain's alarm system goes off. It sees the new behavior as a threat to your established patterns and floods your system with stress hormones. Your willpower—which lives in a part of your brain that tires throughout the day—has to work overtime to fight these natural resistance mechanisms.

It's like trying to swim upstream against a powerful current. You might make progress for a while, but eventually, you'll get exhausted, and the current will carry you back to where you started.

THE POWER OF GOING MICRO

But what if instead of swimming upstream, you found a way to redirect the current itself?

That's exactly what micro-actions do. They're so small that they don't trigger your brain's resistance. They slip under the radar of your inner critic and plant seeds in your neural pathways without setting off any alarms.

Dr. Stephen Maier's research shows that when we experience small, manageable challenges, our brains develop what he calls "learned optimism"—the neural expectation that we can handle whatever comes our way. Each micro-action becomes evidence to your brain that change is possible, safe, and achievable.

Micro-actions aren't "cute."

They're strategic.

Because repetition builds wiring.

Every time you repeat a behavior—no matter how small—you strengthen the neural pathway connected to it. And over time, your brain stops treating that behavior like effort… and starts treating it like default.

THE TRUTH ABOUT HOW CHANGE REALLY HAPPENS

Meaningful change doesn't happen overnight. It doesn't even happen in a week or a month.

The research on habit formation varies widely—some studies suggest weeks, others suggest months—but what matters more than the exact timeline is understanding the natural phases you'll likely experience. Your brain isn't a computer that can be reprogrammed instantly. It's more like a garden that needs time, patience, and consistent care to grow.

The Three Phases of Change You Can Expect

Phase 1: Manual Mode
In the beginning, every micro-action requires conscious effort. You'll forget to do them. You'll remember halfway through the day and feel frustrated. You get annoyed with yourself. That's not failure. That's your brain building new wiring from scratch. It takes mental energy to remember and execute new behaviors.

Phase 2: Repatterning (Building the Groove)
At some point, something shifts. The micro-actions start to feel slightly more natural. You'll still go back to the old ways, but you'll catch yourself sooner. You recover faster. Your brain is beginning to transfer the behavior from conscious control to more automatic processing.

Phase 3: The New Default Mode
Eventually, the micro-actions feel more natural and become an integral part of who you are. You might even feel strange when you

don't do them. Your brain has created neural pathways that support the new behavior, and it requires less conscious effort to maintain. Most people quit in Phase 1 because they misread effort as failure. Effort isn't failure.

Effort is construction.

When You "Slip Back" (And Why It's Actually Normal)

Even after you reach New Default Mode, you might revert to old patterns during high stress, illness, or major life changes.

That doesn't mean you failed. It means you're human.

Dr. Ann Graybiel's research shows habits are stored in specific brain circuits—and stress can pull the brain back toward older, more established patterns. When that happens, your new pathways don't disappear. They just become temporarily less accessible.

So the key isn't perfection.

The key is awareness. When you notice you've slipped back into an old pattern, you now have the neural infrastructure to get back on track more quickly. Each time you return to your micro-actions after a "relapse," you're strengthening your resilience and making the new patterns more robust.

THE THINK FRAMEWORK: YOUR DAILY TOOLKIT FOR CREATING RIPPLES

Let's bring this all together with a practical framework you can use every day. THINK isn't just an acronym—it's a way of rewiring your brain to respond rather than react.

T—Track Your Thoughts

Notice the first story your mind tells you in challenging moments: *They're being difficult. I'm failing. This is unfair.* Just noticing these automatic thoughts weakens their grip on you and gives you space to choose a different response.

Micro-Action: Set three random alarms on your phone. When they go off, simply notice: *What am I thinking right now? How is my body feeling?*

H—Halt Negative Patterns

Use micro-actions as circuit breakers for automatic reactions. The pause between stimulus and response is where your power lives.

Micro-Action: When you notice tension in your body, pause and ask, *What does this moment need from me?*

I—Investigate Your Thoughts

Get curious about your automatic responses instead of judging them. Curiosity activates different neural pathways than anxiety or anger.

Micro-Action: When you have a strong emotional reaction, ask, *What story am I telling myself about this situation? What else might be true?*

N—Nurture New Perspectives

Practice seeing situations from different angles. This builds cognitive flexibility and helps you respond using wisdom instead of wounds.

Micro-Action: When someone annoys you, imagine what might be happening in their life that you can't see. What would make their behavior make sense?

K—Keep Practicing

Remember that neural change happens through repetition, not perfection. Every time you practice a micro-action, you're strengthening the neural pathway.

Micro-Action: At the end of each day, acknowledge one micro-action you practiced, no matter how small. This reinforces the neural pathway and increases the likelihood you'll repeat it tomorrow.

YOUR MICRO-ACTION JOURNEY

Choose one micro-action from this chapter that resonates with you. Start practicing it consistently and track your progress through the three phases. Notice not just how it affects you, but how it affects the people around you.

You're not trying to become perfect. You're trying to become more intentional. You're not trying to change the world overnight. You're trying to change the next moment.

Here are some micro-actions to choose from:

For Morning Routine:

- Take three deep breaths before checking your phone.
- Identify one thing you're grateful for before getting out of bed.
- Set an intention for how you want to show up today.

For Stressful Moments:

- Pause and ask, *what does this moment need from me?*
- Send a kind thought to someone who's frustrating you.
- Take one deep breath before responding to conflict.

For Daily Interactions:

- Make genuine eye contact and smile at one stranger per day.
- Say "thank you" to service workers with real appreciation.
- Listen to understand rather than to respond.

For Evening Reflection:

- Acknowledge one micro-action you practiced today.
- Notice one moment where your presence made a difference.
- Set an intention for tomorrow.

THE RIPPLE THAT STARTS WITH YOU

Your life is built out of ordinary moments.

And in those moments, you're either spreading tension…

Or you're spreading safety.

THINK doesn't make you perfect.

It makes you intentional.

It gives you a way to come back—again and again—until "coming back" becomes your new default.

And once your default changes, the people around you feel it.

When you choose to practice micro-actions, you're becoming a source of calm in a chaotic world. You're creating moments of connection in a disconnected society. You're planting seeds of kindness that will grow in ways you may never see.

That barista you smiled at? They might go home a little lighter and be more patient with their kids. That driver you sent kind thoughts to instead of road rage? They might arrive at their destination a little calmer and treat their family better. That colleague you listened to with genuine curiosity? They might feel seen and valued in a way that changes how they show up for others.

This is how the world changes—not through grand gestures or viral movements, but through millions of tiny moments where people choose connection over disconnection, calm over chaos, and kindness over indifference.

The ripple starts with you. But it doesn't end there.

Take a breath. Take a step. Celebrate your invisible wins. Let's change the world together, one micro-action at a time. Your future self is waiting for your upgraded system.

CHAPTER 15
LEADERSHIP AND COLLECTIVE CHANGE

UPGRADING YOUR INNER OS

I magine walking into your organization and feeling it before anyone says a word.

Not the surface version—the polished town halls, the values on the wall, the engagement survey results. The actual felt experience of being there. Where people speak up because they trust that honesty is safe. Where pressure doesn't make people smaller—it makes them sharper. Where leaders recover quickly, think clearly, and create space for others to do the same. Where performance is sustainable because the people driving it are genuinely well, not performing wellness but operating from a place of real inner strength.

That organization exists, not as a fantasy but as the direct result of leaders who chose to do something most organizations haven't prioritized yet: train the system that is doing all the leading.

This chapter is for you—the person with the power to make that real at scale.

THE OS NOBODY TALKS ABOUT

Every leader is running software—communication styles, decision-making habits, and frameworks for managing people and pressure. The leadership world has given us extraordinary tools to work with.

Stephen Covey gave us principles that outlast trends. Jim Collins showed us what disciplined, humble execution looks like at the highest level. Simon Sinek gave us the power of leading with *why*—purpose as the engine that makes people genuinely want to move. Brené Brown pioneered the understanding that real courage at work means showing up honestly, without the armor. Daniel Goleman brought emotional intelligence into the mainstream. Amy Edmondson built the research case for psychological safety—that teams perform best when it's safe to speak.

These frameworks changed how we think about leadership. And they point, every one of them, toward the person doing the leading.

But there's a layer underneath that rarely gets named.

The Inner OS—your nervous system, your threat-response patterns, your capacity to regulate under pressure and recover afterward—runs constantly, mostly beneath conscious awareness. It is the biological infrastructure underneath everything you do as a leader. And here's what makes it so consequential: it doesn't just affect your performance. It shapes the entire environment in which your people perform.

When your Inner OS is running in chronic threat mode, it doesn't stay contained to your own experience. It surfaces in the assumptions you make under pressure, the people you unconsciously discount, and the ideas you don't hear because your system has already decided the room isn't safe. Your unconscious biases don't operate in a vacuum—they operate through a nervous system. And the people you lead feel the output of that, even when neither of you can name it.

Most leadership development stops at the software. This work goes to the operating system. And that's precisely why it produces results that the other approaches can't fully reach on their own.

YOU ARE AT THE FRONTIER

The leaders and organizations doing this work aren't behind. They're ahead.

The conversation about mental fitness—about training the inner muscles of leadership the same way we train physical performance —is at the frontier of where organizational culture is heading. The science has been building for decades. What's been missing is a framework that makes it accessible, practical, and sustainable inside real organizations with real pressure.

That's exactly what this work offers.

You don't need to overhaul your culture overnight. You don't need a new set of values or a rebranded leadership model. What you need are leaders—starting with you—who understand that the nervous system is organizational infrastructure. And those who are willing to train it accordingly.

The ripple from that decision moves further than most leaders expect.

YOUR SIGNAL IS ALREADY BROADCASTING

We've already established how your nervous system broadcasts into every room you enter. At the organizational level, that signal doesn't just affect one conversation—it sets the emotional climate for an entire team, day after day.

When you walk in feeling regulated, people borrow that steadiness. When you walk in reactively, people brace—often without knowing why. Other brains are reading your face, your voice, and your posture before you've said a word, scanning for one thing: Is it safe to think here? Can I take a risk?

This is signal leadership. It operates whether you're paying attention to it or not.

For leaders who consider themselves results-focused rather than emotionally oriented, this is precisely relevant to you. Your biology is influencing your team's performance regardless. A steadier breath before a hard conversation. A genuine pause before reacting to disappointing news. These aren't softness. They are high-performance inputs—trainable, repeatable, and directly tied to how clearly your team thinks around you.

When you upgrade your Inner OS, you don't just feel better. You create the neurological conditions for your team to access their best thinking. That is the return on inner work.

MENTAL FITNESS: TRAINING THE INNER OS

Early in my career, I worked in education. Parents would come to me with urgency: "My daughter failed the Regents. We have six weeks." The instinct is always to cram everything. That's a trap—and the neuroscience is clear on why.

Instead, we got strategic. We identified the underlying patterns hiding behind the problems. We practiced under real conditions—timed, pressure-tested, and scored without drama. Just data. *Where exactly does the pattern break? Fix that. Run it again.*

We also trained the mind for performance day itself—two slower breaths before opening the booklet, an if-then plan for when her mind went blank, and a first-steps script she could trust when nerves spiked. The result wasn't just a better score. It was a young person who discovered that discomfort doesn't mean danger—and that her inner capacity was something she could actually develop.

When I work with leaders and organizations now, I use the same approach. You don't prepare a strategy and hope your nervous system cooperates when the pressure arrives. You train how you will think, breathe, and recover when it does. You build inner routines you can trust when willpower is thin. You make the uncomfortable familiar—through repetition, not force.

This is mental fitness. Deliberate, consistent training of the inner muscles—applied to the system doing all the leading.

The leaders who hold up best under pressure aren't the ones who feel no stress. They're the ones whose Inner OS has been trained to recover.

RECOGNITION AND APPRECIATION: TWO GEARS, ONE ENGINE

Most leaders believe a sincere "great job" covers the bases. It doesn't —and understanding why is one of the highest-leverage shifts available to any leader.

Recognition and appreciation activate entirely different systems in the brain:

	Recognition	Appreciation
What it addresses	What someone *did*	Who someone *is*
Brain system activated	Dopamine/performance circuitry	Social safety & belonging circuitry
The message it sends	Do more of exactly that	You matter here beyond your output
Example	"Your analysis saved us 4 hours."	"Your calm kept the whole team thinking clearly."

Teams need both consistently. Most organizations are underdelivering on both.

Stop guessing what lands for people. Ask each person on your team their top two ways they feel genuinely valued. Write it down. Then show up the way *they* need, not the way that's easiest for you. Pair recognition and appreciation in the same moment whenever you can.

And watch who gets the spotlight. If the same people keep being seen while others go unacknowledged, you're not building a team— you're building a hierarchy of visibility. The quieter contributors notice. Their nervous systems register it. Over time, their engagement reflects it.

Small and consistent beats grand and occasional. A two-sentence message on a Tuesday— *"The way you handled that situation shifted how I'm thinking about this"*—lands harder than a year-end award. Because it's timely, specific, and human.

SLEEP: THE INFRASTRUCTURE LEADERS CANNOT SHORTCHANGE

This is the conversation most organizations keep deferring—and the one the science says they can't afford to.

Sleep is not a personal preference or a wellness bonus. It is the biological process by which the brain physically clears itself—and without it, leadership capacity doesn't gradually decline. It degrades, quietly, at the cellular level.

In 2013, neuroscientist Maiken Nedergaard discovered the **glymphatic system**—the brain's dedicated overnight clearance network. During sleep, brain cells shrink by approximately 60 percent, opening channels through which cerebrospinal fluid flushes out toxic metabolic waste—

including **beta-amyloid and tau proteins**, the same proteins associated with Alzheimer's disease and neurodegeneration. This process is almost exclusively a sleep function. It barely operates while you're awake.

Matthew Walker's research showed that even a single night of poor sleep produces measurable beta-amyloid accumulation. Chronic sleep deprivation narrows empathy, raises emotional reactivity, and impairs the prefrontal capacities that leadership demands most—judgment, perspective, and the ability to regulate when the stakes are high. One leader's sleep loss ripples through a team: shorter fuse, shakier decisions, lower patience—compounding quietly over months and years.

Sustainable performance isn't built on willpower and caffeine. It's built on brains that have been given what they biologically need to recover, consolidate, and show up fully—day after day, year after year. That's not idealism. That's physiology.

Protecting sleep—consistent timing, morning light, a wind-down that doesn't involve your inbox, prioritizing the nights before high-stakes days—is a performance decision. The organizations that treat it as one will have a measurable edge over the ones that don't.

PSYCHOLOGICAL SAFETY: THE GROUND FLOOR

The highest-performing teams are not the ones with the highest average IQ. They're the ones where it is genuinely safe to say "I don't know," "I got that wrong," or "I have a concern"—without bracing for what comes next.

Edmondson's research is unambiguous: psychological safety is among the strongest predictors of team performance. And safety isn't a cultural vibe. It's biological. When people feel safe, the prefrontal cortex—the seat of focus, creativity, and empathy—stays available. When they don't, the survival brain takes over. You can have the most talented team in the room and still lose access to their best thinking—because the environment made it too costly to offer it.

You build safety through unglamorous, repeatable behaviors:

- Own your mistakes out loud: "I misread that. That's on me."
- Ask, "What's one thing I could do better?"—and actually sit with the answer.
- Meet mistakes with curiosity before judgment: "Walk me through your thinking."
- Recognize learning and effort, not just outcomes

The knowledge of what to do is rarely the gap. Doing it consistently when the pressure is real—that's where the Inner OS either holds or doesn't.

WHAT THIS LOOKS LIKE AT SCALE

When a team practices this work together—not as a one-time training but as a sustained cultural commitment—something measurable shifts.

Meetings feel different. Not softer—sharper. People say the actual thing earlier, which means problems surface faster and solutions emerge with less friction. Leaders who once managed through pressure discover that regulated presence gets faster results than urgency ever did. Recognition and appreciation stop being afterthoughts and start being the consistent signal that tells people their work and their humanity both matter here.

The quieter contributors start speaking. The high performers stop burning out. The leaders who were running on empty start recovering—and their teams feel it immediately.

This isn't a culture transformation program. It's something more durable: leaders, at every level, who understand their own Inner OS well enough to run it on purpose. And when that becomes the norm rather than the exception, the organization doesn't just perform better. It becomes the kind of place people choose to stay, grow, and give their best to.

That culture is built one inner rep at a time. And it starts with the person willing to go first.

THINK AT THE COLLECTIVE LEVEL

Throughout this book, you've been building your THINK practice —training the inner muscles, one rep at a time, until regulation becomes your default rather than your exception.

Now consider what happens when a leader brings that into the culture they're responsible for.

A leader who tracks their first story before responding—rather than reacting—creates the conditions for their team to do the same. A culture that investigates before assigning blame builds the psychological safety that sustains performance through difficulty. A team that receives both recognition and appreciation consistently develops the belonging that keeps people present when things get hard.

THINK scales—not through mandate, but through modeling. When your Inner OS is running clearly, it gives the people around you permission to do their own inner work. Culture isn't built through policy. It's built through the repeated, ordinary moments that accumulate into what an organization actually is—beneath the values on the wall.

———

THE INVITATION

I want to speak directly to you.

You have built something real. You carry the weight of decisions that affect people's livelihoods, their confidence, and their sense of what's possible at work. That is not a small thing.

This work isn't about fixing what's broken. It's about going deeper than the frameworks—beneath the strategy, beneath the communication models, beneath the culture initiatives—to the biological infrastructure running underneath all of it. The layer that, when trained, makes everything else more effective. More sustainable. More human.

The leaders who've committed to this didn't become different people. They became more fully themselves—clearer under pressure, more present in the room, and more capable of creating the conditions where the people around them could think, speak, and show up with everything they've got.

That is the power of a trained Inner OS. A leader who knows how to run their own system—on purpose, under pressure, with consistency—becomes the kind of force that elevates everyone in their orbit. Not through authority alone. Through presence. Through the safety they create without even realizing it. Through the signal they broadcast that says, *"It's safe to think here, it's safe to try, and it's safe to be human at work."*

Stephen Covey, Jim Collins, Simon Sinek, Brené Brown, Daniel Goleman, and Amy Edmondson—they built extraordinary maps. This work is the territory underneath. The nervous system is doing all the leading. The Inner OS is running beneath every strategy, every culture initiative, and every conversation that either builds trust or quietly erodes it.

The Inner OS is already running. The only question is whether you're driving it—or it's driving you.

So my fellow leaders:

Take a breath. Take a step. Lead the way with intention.

CONCLUSION: YOUR INVISIBLE WIN STARTS NOW

WHY THIS BOOK ALMOST NEVER MADE IT TO YOUR HANDS

August 20, 2025, 11:48 p.m.

Wednesday night, and I've been working on writing these final words to you for the past three hours. But I have to admit this book was *supposed* to be finished five months ago.

Actually, I started ideating this book back in November 2024, envisioning a launch that would coincide with New Year themes of hope and fresh starts.

However, my next few months were consumed by a major rebranding project at work, with every ounce of my creative energy poured into it.

Then, the events hit like a freight train. My dad got laid off. My partner and I poured our hearts into our first public initiative, raising mental health awareness in our community, honoring the lives we'd lost, and trying to build something meaningful from our grief.

Through it all, the voice in my head kept getting louder: *You're falling behind on your book. What's wrong with you?*

Through writing this book, though, I've learned that life doesn't care about your timeline. I've learned that you can't pour from an empty cup when your full-time job demands every ounce of your creative energy. I've learned that you can't write about mental fitness while managing family crises, career demands, and community initiatives. You can't weave stories about your assault without reliving every painful detail, draining your emotional reserves night after night.

You can't write consistently while recovering from neck surgery, learning to navigate physical therapy sessions, and rebuilding your strength one day at a time.

But you know what kept me going through every delayed deadline, every moment when I wanted to quit? The thought of you. You, reading this at 3 a.m., wondering if life is worth living. You, who feels trapped with no way out. You, who thinks you're the only one fighting invisible battles.

Three men in my community took their own lives last year. One was from my local gym. Everyone who knew him said they didn't see the signs. *He seemed fine. He looked like he had it together.*

Unfortunately, too many of us don't have support when we need it most. But all it takes is one person to show you that you freaking matter.

That's why this book exists.

I know I can't help everyone. But I can help someone. And if these words reach that one person who needs to know they're not alone, that there is a way through, that their invisible battles matter—then every late night, every delayed deadline, every moment of doubt was worth it.

HERE'S WHAT I NEED YOU TO REMEMBER

After everything we've covered in these pages—from understanding your brain's wiring to reframing your relationship with stress, from building emotional regulation to creating sustainable habits—it all comes down to this:

Your invisible battles matter. Your quiet victories count. And showing up however you can is enough.

I used to believe we needed to be mentally tough. But through everything I've been through, I've realized it's more important that we become mentally **fit**.

Mental toughness says: *Push through no matter what.*

Mental fitness says: *Work with your biology, not against it.*

Mental toughness says: *Weakness is failure.*

Mental fitness says: *Rest is part of the training.*

Mental toughness says: *Handle it alone.*

Mental fitness says: *Community makes you stronger.*

YOU ARE NOT ALONE IN THIS

I see you there, reading this at 2 a.m. because that's the only quiet time you get. I see you pushing through another day with a smile after a 16-plus-hour shift at work, fighting battles no one else can see. I see you wondering if you're strong enough, smart enough, and resilient enough to handle what life keeps throwing at you.

I see you because I am you. I've been where you are—questioning everything, feeling behind, wondering if I'm doing enough, being enough, and healing fast enough. But your pace is your pace. Your journey is your journey. And your willingness to keep going, even when it's messy and slow and nothing like you planned—that's where your real strength lives.

WHAT'S POSSIBLE FOR YOU NOW

You've absorbed neuroscience. You understand how your brain works. You have the tools for emotional regulation, stress reframing, and habit building. But knowledge without action is just expensive entertainment.

So here's what I want for you:

- I want you to stop measuring your worth by other people's timelines.
- I want you to see that your pace is your pace, and it's perfect for your journey.
- I want you to celebrate the invisible wins—the morning you got out of bed despite depression, the meeting you attended while grieving, and the smile you gave someone while carrying your own pain.

- I want you to build your mental fitness like you'd build physical fitness—consistently, patiently, with rest days built in.
- I want you to know that seeking help is strength, not weakness.
- I want you to join a movement that's just getting started, where your story matters.

Most importantly, I want you to become the inner leader of your own life.

If you are ready to train this, not just understand it, here is what to do next.

WORK WITH ME

I help high achievers become high performers, so success stops costing your nervous system, your relationships, and your peace.

This is not the end of your journey. If you want, we can keep building together.

1. Start Here: The Stress and Overwhelm Reality Check

A short science-backed assessment that shows how stress is showing up in your life and what to focus on first.

Best for: *"I need clarity before I change anything."*

271

2. The Mind Gym

A guided training experience designed to turn the concepts in this book into real-life habits through simple, repeatable reps.

Best for: *"I'm ready to train this—consistently."*

3. Coaching

One-on-one support for high-stakes seasons that require privacy, precision, and a custom plan.

Best for: "I'm done coping. My situation is complex, and I want targeted support."

IMPORTANT DISCLAIMER

I am a neuroscientist and a high-performance mental fitness coach, not a licensed therapist. This program is not therapy, nor is it a substitute for clinical mental health treatment. While this experience may support emotional awareness, mindset shifts, nervous system regulation, and a foundation for mental well-being, it is a coaching-based experience, not a therapeutic one. If you are currently experiencing severe distress, trauma, or symptoms that require clinical care, I strongly encourage you to seek support from a licensed mental health professional.

You deserve the right kind of support at the right time.

TAKE YOUR FIRST STEP NOW: JOIN THE MOVEMENT

This isn't the end of our journey together. It's the beginning of a movement to create a community of invisible winners. This movement starts right here, right now, with you and me. Together, we're creating something that didn't exist before: a place where invisible winners finally get seen, heard, and celebrated.

Do not overthink this.

Share one invisible win.

One moment, you caught yourself. One reset you used. One choice that protected your peace. It counts.

Post it with the following hashtags:

#WeAreInvisibleWinners #InvisibleWinsMovement #MentalFitness #InnerLeader

Or share your story on our site.

Because your invisible wins deserve to be seen.

Start here: invisible-winners.com

ACKNOWLEDGMENTS

Whose flexibility made this book possible:

Mia and my Game Changer Publishing team (Cris, Rasika, and Nicole)—you believed in this book through every delay. Ninety days became nine months as I navigated my dad's layoff, my own layoff, recovery from neck surgery, and the loss of my companion, Iri. Through the emotionally draining work of speaking my trauma out loud and navigating the challenges of 2025, you never made me feel "behind"—you simply held the door open while I did the work the mission required.

To Debbie, Jessica, and Tracy from the editing team, and to the rest of the proofreading and Julia from the formatting team—thank you for the quiet but powerful role you played in bringing this book forward. Your care, detail, and commitment helped ensure this message could be carried with clarity, strength, and heart.

Skylar—thank you for your incredible talent as a designer. You took the heart of my message and brought it to life on the cover, giving the invisible wins a face the world can finally see.

Whose teaching became my foundation:

Ben Newman—your Coach to Coaches program was the spark I needed to finally solidify my years of learning and expertise into something tangible and transformative. To me, you have always been "always in, in a heartbeat"—accessible, intentional, authentic, and humble. Thank you for investing your time in us in such a meaningful way.

PJ Milani—your Visual Metaphor class fundamentally changed how I think about visual messages and gave me the tools to make the abstract visible. Your guidance helped me think more deeply, create more intentionally, and communicate beyond words alone.

My fellow creatives from PJ's class—Eva, Gordon, and members of cohorts 13 and 14—thank you for your honest feedback on some of the early visual concepts I explored for this book. Your perspectives helped me think more critically and refine my direction through the many iterations that followed.

Whose community became my mission:

Mike Orrechio—for believing in our mission and giving us the space at Basecamp to launch our first public initiative, celebrating the quiet battles of invisible winners.

Coach Brian from Basecamp—your tireless advocacy for mental health awareness and your heart for this community go above and beyond anything I could have asked for.

Jorge A, my fellow Basecamper—we connected through a shared passion for men's mental health, and your constant check-ins and championship of this book have been a true gift.

Whose kindness reminded me I wasn't invisible:

Nicola—after the assault, when I felt most unseen, you checked in. Small acts of humanity like yours are the reason people survive their darkest seasons.

Josh—thank you for being human with me during one of the hardest periods of my life. Your support reminded me that I mattered.

Pastor Andy—you have a rare gift for seeing the pain in my eyes even when I am smiling. Thank you for truly seeing me and for the love you pour into everyone you meet.

Whose battle set me on this path:

My grandfather—your struggle with Alzheimer's was the seed of my PhD and my obsession with the brain. Everything I have researched started with the hope of understanding you.

Whose love anchored me through the darkest years:

My sister—you held our family together when I couldn't hold myself. You are the invisible winner I have always looked up to.

Dan—you are the kind of man who doesn't need to say "I love you" because you show it every single day through your actions. You stayed through the ugly times, through thick and thin, and through the years that tried to break me. You were the anchor I needed when the world felt too heavy to stay in.

Iri—10.5 years of following me everywhere, the silent witness to my deepest grief and my greatest joys. The house is too quiet without you on the couch, but I carry your unconditional love with me every day. Thank you for staying with me, queen of the house. Run free, my Iri gal.

Whose invisible sacrifice shaped me:

My dad—working night shifts 7 days a week in the freezing cold— you showed me that fear is squashed by a mission larger than yourself: fighting for the ones you love. You gave me the courage to learn a new language and create a life I never thought possible.

My mom—you always know when something is wrong before I even speak. Your quiet, steady presence is the foundation I built my strength upon.

My grandmother—you taught me the most vital lesson of survival: just take the next breath, then the next, then the next.

Whose invisible battles I fight for:

Every person reading this—you are an invisible winner. Your quiet battle counts. Your story matters. You are not alone.

Whose breath sustained me:

God—for giving me the courage to keep breathing when I wanted to stop and for transforming my deepest pain into my highest purpose.

And for those reading this who may not share my faith—may you find the Higher Power or inner light that sustains you through your own darkest nights.

I am alive so that I can save someone else's life.
I am alive so that I can shine the light for
that (1) person going through hell.

I am alive so that I can support that (1) person
who needs someone to listen.

Let my life not be in vain

This Book is my invisible win.

If it helps even (1) person feel less alone,
then every painful moment that led me here was worth it.

Your Inner Champion.
Your Friendly Neighborhood Brain Whisperer,

Khai Win

May you find your Iri in this Lifetime,
A Reminder that even in the hardest seasons,
tenderness still existts.
In Loving memory of Iri♡

FURTHER READINGS

Stress physiology, survival mode, and allostatic load

McEwen, B. S. (1998). Protective and damaging effects of stress mediators. *The New England Journal of Medicine, 338*(3), 171–179. https://doi.org/10.1056/NEJM199801153380307

McEwen, B. S., & Stellar, E. (1993). Stress and the individual: Mechanisms leading to disease. *Archives of Internal Medicine, 153*(18), 2093–2101.

Sapolsky, R. M. (2004). *Why zebras don't get ulcers* (3rd ed.). Henry Holt.

Sterling, P., & Eyer, J. (1988). Allostasis: A new paradigm to explain arousal pathology. In S. Fisher & J. Reason (Eds.), *Handbook of life stress, cognition, and health* (pp. 629–649). Wiley.

Trauma, PTSD, memory fragmentation, and nervous system stabilization (incl. "window of tolerance")

American Psychiatric Association. (2022). *Diagnostic and statistical manual of mental disorders* (5th ed., text rev.; DSM-5-TR). Author.

Brewin, C. R., Dalgleish, T., & Joseph, S. (1996). A dual representation theory of posttraumatic stress disorder. *Psychological Review, 103*(4), 670–686. https://doi.org/10.1037/0033-295X.103.4.670

Ehlers, A., & Clark, D. M. (2000). A cognitive model of posttraumatic stress disorder. *Behaviour Research and Therapy, 38*(4), 319–345. https://doi.org/10.1016/S0005-7967(99)00123-0

Herman, J. L. (1992). *Trauma and recovery*. Basic Books.

van der Kolk, B. A. (1994). The body keeps the score: Memory and the evolving psychobiology of posttraumatic stress. *Harvard Review of Psychiatry, 1*(5), 253–265. https://doi.org/10.3109/10673229409017088

van der Kolk, B. A. (2014). *The body keeps the score: Brain, mind, and body in the healing of trauma*. Viking.

Epigenetics, adversity, and intergenerational transmission ("written in our cells")

McGowan, P. O., Sasaki, A., D'Alessio, A. C., Dymov, S., Labonté, B., Szyf, M., Turecki, G., & Meaney, M. J. (2009). Epigenetic regulation of the glucocorticoid receptor in human brain associates with childhood abuse. *Nature Neuroscience, 12*, 342–348. https://doi.org/10.1038/nn.2270

Weaver, I. C. G., Cervoni, N., Champagne, F. A., D'Alessio, A. C., Sharma, S., Seckl, J. R., Dymov, S., Szyf, M., & Meaney, M. J. (2004). Epigenetic programming by maternal behavior. *Nature Neuroscience, 7*, 847–854. https://doi.org/10.1038/nn1276

Yehuda, R., Daskalakis, N. P., Bierer, L. M., Bader, H. N., Klengel, T., Holsboer, F., & Binder, E. B. (2016). Holocaust exposure induced intergenerational effects on FKBP5 methylation. *Biological Psychiatry, 80*(5), 372–380. https://doi.org/10.1016/j.biopsych.2015.08.005

Thought awareness, metacognition, and default mode activity (rumination/autopilot)

Raichle, M. E., MacLeod, A. M., Snyder, A. Z., Powers, W. J., Gusnard, D. A., & Shulman, G. L. (2001). A default mode of brain function. *Proceedings of the National Academy of Sciences, 98*(2), 676–682. https://doi.org/10.1073/pnas.98.2.676

Whitfield-Gabrieli, S., & Ford, J. M. (2012). Default mode network activity and connectivity in psychopathology. *Annual Review of Clinical Psychology, 8*, 49–76. https://doi.org/10.1146/annurev-clinpsy-032511-143049

Negativity bias, threat prioritization, and rapid affective processing

Baumeister, R. F., Bratslavsky, E., Finkenauer, C., & Vohs, K. D. (2001). Bad is stronger than good. *Review of General Psychology, 5*(4), 323–370. https://doi.org/10.1037/1089-2680.5.4.323

Rozin, P., & Royzman, E. B. (2001). Negativity bias, negativity dominance, and contagion. *Personality and Social Psychology Review, 5*(4), 296–320. https://doi.org/10.1207/S15327957PSPR0504_2

Emotion regulation, affect labeling ("name it to tame it"), and cognitive reappraisal

Gross, J. J. (1998). The emerging field of emotion regulation: An integrative review. *Review of General Psychology, 2*(3), 271–299. https://doi.org/10.1037/1089-2680.2.3.271

Lieberman, M. D., Eisenberger, N. I., Crockett, M. J., Tom, S. M., Pfeifer, J. H., & Way, B. M. (2007). Putting feelings into words: Affect labeling disrupts amygdala activity in response to affective stimuli. *Psychological Science, 18*(5), 421–428. https://doi.org/10.1111/j.1467-9280.2007.01916.x

Ochsner, K. N., & Gross, J. J. (2005). The cognitive control of emotion. *Trends in Cognitive Sciences, 9*(5), 242–249. https://doi.org/10.1016/j.tics.2005.03.010

Mindfulness/meditation (secular applications) and mental health outcomes

Goyal, M., Singh, S., Sibinga, E. M. S., et al. (2014). Meditation programs for psychological stress and well-being: A systematic review and meta-analysis. *JAMA Internal Medicine, 174*(3), 357–368. https://doi.org/10.1001/jamainternmed.2013.13018

Hölzel, B. K., Lazar, S. W., Gard, T., Schuman-Olivier, Z., Vago, D. R., & Ott, U. (2011). How does mindfulness meditation work? Proposing mechanisms of action from a conceptual and neural perspective. *Perspectives on Psychological Science, 6*(6), 537–559. https://doi.org/10.1177/1745691611419671

Kabat-Zinn, J. (1990). *Full catastrophe living*. Delacorte.

Breathing practices, autonomic regulation, vagal pathways, and HRV

Balban, M. Y., Naranjo, D. E., Caldwell, J. L., et al. (2023). Brief structured respiration practices enhance mood and reduce physiological arousal. *Cell Reports Medicine, 4*(1), 100895. https://doi.org/10.1016/j.xcrm.2022.100895

Shaffer, F., & Ginsberg, J. P. (2017). An overview of heart rate variability metrics and norms. *Frontiers in Public Health, 5*, 258. https://doi.org/10.3389/fpubh.2017.00258

Thayer, J. F., Åhs, F., Fredrikson, M., Sollers, J. J., III, & Wager, T. D. (2012). A meta-analysis of heart rate variability and neuroimaging studies: Implications for heart rate variability as a marker of stress and health. *Neuroscience & Biobehavioral Reviews, 36*(2), 747–756. https://doi.org/10.1016/j.neubiorev.2011.11.009

Zaccaro, A., Piarulli, A., Laurino, M., Garbella, E., Menicucci, D., Neri, B., & Gemignani, A. (2018). How breath-control can change your life: A systematic review on psychophysiological correlates of slow breathing. *Frontiers in Human Neuroscience, 12,* 353. https://doi.org/10.3389/fnhum.2018.00353

Tiny habits, behavior change, and implementation intentions ("small steps, massive freedom")

Fogg, B. J. (2019). *Tiny habits: The small changes that change everything.* Houghton Mifflin Harcourt.

Gollwitzer, P. M. (1999). Implementation intentions: Strong effects of simple plans. *American Psychologist, 54*(7), 493–503. https://doi.org/10.1037/0003-066X.54.7.493

Gollwitzer, P. M., & Sheeran, P. (2006). Implementation intentions and goal achievement: A meta-analysis of effects and processes. *Advances in Experimental Social Psychology, 38,* 69–119. https://doi.org/10.1016/S0065-2601(06)38002-1

Lally, P., van Jaarsveld, C. H. M., Potts, H. W. W., & Wardle, J. (2010). How are habits formed: Modelling habit formation in the real world. *European Journal of Social Psychology, 40*(6), 998–1009. https://doi.org/10.1002/ejsp.674

Wood, W., & Neal, D. T. (2007). A new look at habits and the habit-goal interface. *Psychological Review, 114*(4), 843–863. https://doi.org/10.1037/0033-295X.114.4.843

Newman, B. (2023). *The standard: Winning every day at your highest level.* Game Changer Publishing.

Dopamine, reward learning, and reinforcement loops (motivation/celebration)

Berridge, K. C., & Robinson, T. E. (1998). What is the role of dopamine in reward: Hedonic impact, reward learning, or incentive salience? *Brain Research Reviews, 28*(3), 309–369. https://doi.org/10.1016/S0165-0173(98)00019-8

Schultz, W. (1997). Dopamine neurons and their role in reward mechanisms. *Current Opinion in Neurobiology, 7*(2), 191–197. https://doi.org/10.1016/S0959-4388(97)80007-4

Wise, R. A. (2004). Dopamine, learning and motivation. *Nature Reviews Neuroscience, 5*, 483–494. https://doi.org/10.1038/nrn1406

Neuroplasticity, learning (LTP/LTD), myelin, and practice

Bliss, T. V. P., & Lømo, T. (1973). Long-lasting potentiation of synaptic transmission in the dentate area of the anaesthetized rabbit following stimulation of the perforant path. *The Journal of Physiology, 232*(2), 331–356. https://doi.org/10.1113/jphysiol.1973.sp010273

Draganski, B., Gaser, C., Busch, V., Schuierer, G., Bogdahn, U., & May, A. (2004). Neuroplasticity: Changes in grey matter induced by training. *Nature, 427*, 311–312. https://doi.org/10.1038/427311a

Fields, R. D. (2008). White matter in learning, cognition and psychiatric disorders. *Trends in Neurosciences, 31*(7), 361–370. https://doi.org/10.1016/j.tins.2008.04.001

Hebb, D. O. (1949). *The organization of behavior: A neuropsychological theory.* Wiley.

Zatorre, R. J., Fields, R. D., & Johansen-Berg, H. (2012). Plasticity in gray and white: Neuroimaging changes in brain structure during learning. *Nature Neuroscience, 15,* 528–536. https://doi.org/10.1038/nn.3045

Sleep, recovery, and cognitive/emotional stability

Diekelmann, S., & Born, J. (2010). The memory function of sleep. *Nature Reviews Neuroscience, 11,* 114–126. https://doi.org/10.1038/nrn2762

Walker, M. (2017). *Why we sleep: Unlocking the power of sleep and dreams.* Scribner.

Social connection, co-regulation, synchrony, and social pain

Coan, J. A. (2011). The social regulation of emotion. *American Psychologist, 66*(4), 276–287. https://doi.org/10.1037/a0022720

Eisenberger, N. I., Lieberman, M. D., & Williams, K. D. (2003). Does rejection hurt? An fMRI study of social exclusion. *Science, 302*(5643), 290–292. https://doi.org/10.1126/science.1089134

Burnout, workplace toxicity/incivility, and psychological safety

Andersson, L. M., & Pearson, C. M. (1999). Tit for tat? The spiraling effect of incivility in the workplace. *Academy of Management Review, 24*(3), 452–471. https://doi.org/10.2307/259136

Edmondson, A. (1999). Psychological safety and learning behavior in work teams. *Administrative Science Quarterly, 44*(2), 350–383. https://doi.org/10.2307/2666999

Maslach, C., Schaufeli, W. B., & Leiter, M. P. (2001). Job burnout. *Annual Review of Psychology, 52,* 397–422. https://doi.org/10.1146/annurev.psych.52.1.397

Bias, "dangerous shortcuts," and judgment under uncertainty

Greenwald, A. G., & Banaji, M. R. (1995). Implicit social cognition: Attitudes, self-esteem, and stereotypes. *Psychological Review, 102*(1), 4–27. https://doi.org/10.1037/0033-295X.102.1.4

Kahneman, D. (2011). *Thinking, fast and slow.* Farrar, Straus and Giroux.

Tversky, A., & Kahneman, D. (1974). Judgment under uncertainty: Heuristics and biases. *Science, 185*(4157), 1124–1131. https://doi.org/10.1126/science.185.4157.1124

Men, stigma, and help-seeking

Addis, M. E., & Mahalik, J. R. (2003). Men, masculinity, and the contexts of help seeking. *American Psychologist, 58*(1), 5–14. https://doi.org/10.1037/0003-066X.58.1.5

Seidler, Z. E., Dawes, A. J., Rice, S. M., Oliffe, J. L., & Dhillon, H. M. (2016). The role of masculinity in men's help-seeking for depression: A systematic review. *Clinical Psychology Review, 49,* 106–118. https://doi.org/10.1016/j.cpr.2016.09.002

Suicide: theory, risk, and prevention frameworks

Joiner, T. (2005). *Why people die by suicide.* Harvard University Press.

Klonsky, E. D., & May, A. M. (2015). The three-step theory (3ST): A new theory of suicide rooted in the "ideation-to-action" framework. *International Journal of Cognitive Therapy, 8*(2), 114–129. https://doi.org/10.1521/ijct.2015.8.2.114

O'Connor, R. C. (2011). The integrated motivational–volitional model of suicidal behavior. *Crisis, 32*(6), 295–298. https://doi.org/10.1027/0227-5910/a000120

Stanley, B., & Brown, G. K. (2012). Safety planning intervention: A brief intervention to mitigate suicide risk. *Cognitive and Behavioral Practice, 19*(2), 256–264. https://doi.org/10.1016/j.cbpra.2011.01.001

Meaning-making, choice, and post-traumatic growth

Frankl, V. E. (2006). *Man's search for meaning.* Beacon Press. (Original work published 1946)

Park, C. L. (2010). Making sense of the meaning literature: An integrative review of meaning making and its effects on adjustment to stressful life events. *Psychological Bulletin, 136*(2), 257–301. https://doi.org/10.1037/a0018301

Tedeschi, R. G., & Calhoun, L. G. (2004). Posttraumatic growth: Conceptual foundations and empirical evidence. *Psychological Inquiry, 15*(1), 1–18.

Works explicitly referenced in the manuscript (memoir/literary/philosophical anchors)

Angelou, M. (1969). *I know why the caged bird sings.* Random House.

Aurelius, M. (2002). *Meditations* (G. Hays, Trans.). Modern Library.

Baldwin, J. (1955). *Notes of a native son.* Beacon Press.

Jung, C. G. (2009). *The Red Book: Liber Novus* (S. Shamdasani, Ed.; M. Kyburz, J. Peck, & S. Shamdasani, Trans.). W. W. Norton & Company.

Nguyen, J. (2022.). *Don't believe everything you think: Why your thinking is the beginning & end of suffering.*

Newman, B. (2023). *The standard.*

Woolf, V. (2025). *A room of one's own.* Hogarth Press.

THANK YOU FOR READING MY BOOK!

You took a chance on these pages. I don't take that lightly. I'd love to connect with you personally

Scan the QR Code:

I appreciate your interest in my book and value your feedback, as it helps me improve future versions.

Thank you!

www.ingramcontent.com/pod-product-compliance
Lightning Source LLC
Chambersburg PA
CBHW032045280526
45784CB00011B/2781